Smoking, Curing & Drying

The Complete Guide for Meat & Fish

All the my best

P. P. Turan 2017

First published in the UK in 2015 by
APPLE PRESS
74–77 White Lion Street
London N1 9PF
United Kingdom

www.apple-press.com

ISBN 978-1-84543-561-5

Printed in China by 1010 Printing International Ltd.
9 8 7 6 5 4 3 2

This book was conceived, designed and produced by
Quantum Books Limited
6 Blundell Street
London N7 9BH
United Kingdom

Publisher: Kerry Enzor
Project Editor: Cathy Meeus
Design: Louise Turpin
Cover design: Gareth Butterworth
Proofreader: Jane Bamforth
Indexer: Diana LeCore
Photography: Simon Pask
Production Manager: Rohana Yusof
Consultant: Matthew McClune

QUMPRME

Smoking, Curing & Drying

The Complete Guide for Meat & Fish

Turan T. Turan

APPLE

Contents

Curing: Preserving with Salt

69

42

96

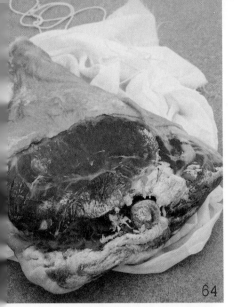

64

52

79

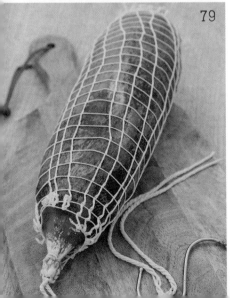

Drying Meat and Fish

Smoking Meat and Fish

Resources

Foreword

Salting, brining, drying, and smoking are as much a part of our food heritage as the traditional skills of hunting and farming. These food preservation practices are at risk of falling into a category of forgotten arts – being replaced by readily available, mass-produced versions that are cheaper to make. Yet I believe these timeless techniques should be preserved, adapted where necessary, and passed down through the generations. Not to mention that food made with these long-perfected techniques simply tastes much, much better!

For me, preserving meat and fish is something that first prompted my interest as a young man when I used to go sea fishing and ended up having to throw away most of my catch due to spoilage. It wasn't until I tried to create traditional Scottish smoked salmon that I really started to explore this wonderful craft, and the alchemy of the process of salting, brining, and smoking slowly revealed itself to me. I've been lucky; I come from a food-obsessed family who have been involved in the restaurant and food business for most of their lives – so I grew up with an appreciation for gourmet cooking. While my own career path took a completely different direction – I served for over 30 years as a firefighter in London – my parent's passion for good food seems to have rubbed off on me and I now run one-day food preservation and smoking courses to share my love of these unique, artisan crafts. Even in retirement I can't help but come home smelling of smoke.

Exploring food and the processes associated with deepening flavour fascinate me. I also love science, and combining my fascination for the chemical processes behind salting, brining, drying, and smoking meat with my love for food is a truly wonderful "marriage" of enthusiasms. This book describes some significant stages in my journey into food preservation and smoking. I would like to think these stepping stones can act as a guide for you along your own journey into this extraordinary and rewarding craft.

This book is for everyone who has an interest in what goes into their food. It is not just about trying to make food last longer; if that's your goal then just put your food in the refrigerator or freezer and you're done. The processes explained in this book are intended to capture the interest of those who want to transform their ingredients with improved texture and tenderness, deeper flavours and interesting scents, and beautiful natural colouring. You will learn how to use these ancient processes to create some of the most sought-after delicacies in the modern culinary repertoire, and which new techniques make preserving meat and fish easily achievable in a modern kitchen. I would like this book to inspire you to expand your own culinary ambitions.

It's true that traditional food preservation techniques evolved through the need to provide food for families and whole communities all through the year. Today that need has changed for most people, but our desire to serve delicious food remains just as strong. I can think of no better reason for wanting to learn these skills than the sheer delight of seeing people you love enjoying the uniquely flavoursome produce you have created using these artisan techniques.

My advice to you, the reader, is to start with a dish that ignites your passion and whets your appetite, and see how you get on. Remember, every journey starts with just one step and I hope this book will set you going in a new and exciting direction.

Good luck!

Turan T. Turan

How to Use This Book

The book is organized into three main sections corresponding to the broad categories of technique that are used for preserving meat and fish. The arrangement of the book is intended to make it easy for the reader to understand the order of the key processes for preserving meat and fish and will help you to find the information you need quickly.

Techniques for preparing different meat and fish products have been assigned to a particular section according to the principal method of preservation used. But because many products involve more that one process, there are helpful cross-references to enable you to find further information as needed.

CURING: PRESERVING WITH SALT

This is the first part of the book and it covers this very important step in the preserving process. Salting – either dry-salting or brining (soaking in a salt solution) is the first stage in the production of most preserved foods, and is generally followed by one or both of the processes described in the other two parts of the book.

DRYING MEAT AND FISH

This chapter of the book deals with drying – the removal of excess moisture. Most preserved meat and fish is subject to a drying process – usually carried out after salting and before smoking (if required).

SMOKING MEAT AND FISH

Smoking is the culmination of the preservation process for some foods and is therefore the last technique to be described. Smoking includes both cold smoking, in which the smoke provides flavour but insufficient heat to cook the food, and hot smoking in which the food is cooked by – as well as being flavoured by – the smoke.

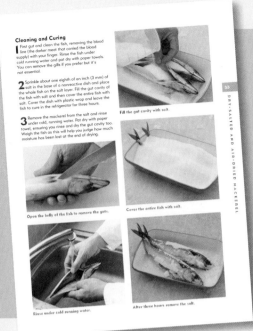

STEP-BY-STEP GUIDANCE

Geared to meet the needs of the reader who wants to use the techniques at home, each technique is explained in easy-to-follow stages, with accompanying photographs and illustrations. Where necessary, there are cross-references to other parts of the book in which specific aspects of the process are explained in more detail.

Helpful lists of the ingredients you will need and information panels that provide useful tips are included to give more detail on particular aspects of the process.

TIPS AND TECHNIQUES

The book aims to provide you with sufficient understanding to apply the techniques creatively using a variety of ingredients. Advice is provided on using each technique for different foods. And there are useful tips throughout the book for making a success of the projects you undertake.

RECIPES GALORE

Once you've learned how to prepare and preserve different cuts of meat and types of fish, you'll need ideas for how to serve these delicacies to your family and friends. Throughout the book you'll find exciting and delicious recipes and serving suggestions.

ADDITIONAL INFORMATION

The final pages of the book are devoted to a useful resources section that lists suppliers of equipment and other specialist items that you may need. There is also a full glossary of specialist terms, and a comprehensive index to help you find your way.

Introduction to Preserving

Why do we need to preserve meat and fish? Of course these techniques make our food last longer, but preserving is about more than that. We preserve meat and fish because we love the unique flavours and textures that the processes create, using simple, natural additives such as salt and herbs. The process of preserving using salt, drying, and smoking transforms good food into great food. There's also a great deal of satisfaction to be had from producing your own cured foods for your charcuterie platter.

Scope of the Book

This book covers the three important areas of the preservation of meat and fish: preserving with salt, drying, and smoking, which are age-old processes and techniques that hold a special interest for me. These processes complement each other, and while being individual methods in their own right, they are often used in combination. Brining or salting food is a key stage of the drying and smoking methods too, either removing excess moisture from the meat or actually helping meat to stay moist and succulent during processes like hot smoking. Salting, drying, and smoking all work together to transform your food into a wide range of delicacies.

The flow charts on the following pages explain how the different salting methods fit into the various preservation processes covered in this book.

Salt is used to cure pork for bacon: the salt helps to extract moisture from the meat.

SALT: THE COMMON INGREDIENT

Salt or, to give it its chemical name, sodium chloride (NaCl) is key to all the processes in this book. Salt fulfills two main functions. First, it discourages the growth of bacteria and, secondly, salt has the effect of drawing moisture from meat and fish, making the environment even more hostile for bacteria and other germs. You'll learn more about the action of salt on page 18.

All meat and fish need to be treated with salt – a process known as curing – as part of the preservation procedure. Curing is achieved through brining – in which the meat or fish is soaked in a salt and water solution (brine) – or by dry curing – the application of dry salt to the outside of the meat or fish. The flow charts on these pages show how curing with dry salt or brine fits into the sequences of processes for each method of preservation covered in this book: salting, drying, and smoking.

SALTING METHODS

WHAT IS SALTING?

THE TECHNIQUE
Salt or brine is applied to the meat or fish, which is then left to cure.

THE PROCESS
The salt draws out moisture. The aim is for a weight loss of 5–15 per cent. The salt inhibits bacterial growth.

THE RESULT
Texture becomes firmer and colour deepens. Flavours are enhanced and storage life extended.

BRINING

START

ADD HERBS, SPICES, AND SWEETENERS

Submerge in water and salt solution (brine)

Minimal moisture loss: texture becomes firmer

Rinse, dry, and use for an additional process or slow roast

DRY SALTING

ADD HERBS, SPICES, AND SWEETENERS

Apply dry salt to meat

Significant moisture loss: texture becomes firmer

Further moisture loss: sticky coating (pellicle) forms on surface

Rinse, dry, and serve or use for an additional process

CURING

FINISH

SALTING/BRINING

Brining is a key stage when making salt beef (page 38) and pastrami (page 42).

DRYING

Drying is the main curing process used for pancetta (page 106).

SMOKING

Smoking is used to create favourites like Scottish-style cold-smoked salmon (page 158).

DRYING METHODS

WHAT IS DRYING?

THE TECHNIQUE
Meat or fish is marinated in flavourings or treated with dry salt. It is then dried or further cured and then dried.

THE PROCESS
Meat and fish can be dried naturally or mechanically using additional heat. Drying reduces weight by 50 per cent or more.

THE RESULT
Texture becomes firmer and colour deepens. Flavours are enhanced and storage life extended.

PREPARATION

SLICE THICK
(For biltong)

SLICE THIN
(For jerky)

RETAIN WHOLE MUSCLE OR CUT OF MEAT
(For bresaola, etc.)

ADD HERBS, SPICES, AND SWEETENERS

Marinating

Loss of moisture, texture becomes firmer

ADD ADDITIONAL HERBS
(for biltong)

Drying

Use forced methods: dehydrator, oven, or biltong box

Use natural methods: sun or air drying

CURING

DRYING

ADD HERBS, SPICES, AND SWEETENERS

Dry salting

Loss of moisture, texture becomes firmer

ADDITIONAL HERBS AND SPICES

WRAPPING, TYING, AND HANGING

Drying

Use a conditioning room, dry in natural cool air, or use dry-aging bags

Understanding the Terminology

SALTING
Sometimes referred to as pre-salting, this is the application of salt to a piece of fish or meat as the initial stage of the preservation process. Salting may be followed by a process of drying or smoking. Salting differs from seasoning mainly due to the larger quantity of salt used in the process. See also Brining and Dry Salting (right).

DRY SALTING
This is a salting process that involves covering the meat or fish in salt for a period of hours or days. This is used for making a wide variety of cured meats and fish, such as bacon, bresaola, prosciutto, and salt cod. This process is commonly referred to as applying a "rub" to the meat.

BRINING
The process of immersing meat or fish in a solution of salt and water to preserve the food, a "wet" curing method. The brine can include added herbs, spices, vinegars, and sweeteners.

CURING
A generic term that can be used to describe preserving processes that use salt. A cured meat or fish product is one that has been produced using salting, drying, or smoking — or a combination of these techniques.

SMOKING METHODS

WHAT IS SMOKING?

THE TECHNIQUE
Meat or fish is initially prepared with dry salt or brine and then exposed to smoke. In hot smoking, the salt is mainly for seasoning purposes; in cold smoking it is for preservation.

THE PROCESS
Wood smoke is applied to fish or meat. In hot smoking heat is applied at the same time to cook or change the structure of the meat.

THE RESULT
Texture becomes firmer and colour deepens. Flavours are enhanced and, in the case of cold smoking, storage life is extended.

COLD SMOKING	PREPARATION	HOT SMOKING

ADD HERBS, SPICES, AND SWEETENERS		ADD HERBS, SPICES, AND SWEETENERS
Brining or dry salting		Brining or dry salting
Loss of moisture, texture becomes firmer	**CURING**	Less moisture loss required; texture becomes firmer
Further loss of moisture; sticky coating (pellicle) forms	**DRYING**	
Smoke below 86°F (30°C): further loss of moisture	**SMOKING**	BASTE
		Smoke above 72°C (162°F): product cooks slowly maintaining moisture
After up to 48 hrs in the smoker: further drying; colour darkens; texture firms still further	**FINISH**	After up to 12 hours in the smoke and heat: meat becomes tender and colour darkens

CURE
A mixture consisting primarily of salt that is applied to meat or fish as part of the preservation process. It also may include other flavourings such as herbs and spices, and small amounts of chemical preservatives such as nitrates and nitrites found in Prague Powders (see Preservatives, page 25).

MARINATING
The application of a mixture of various herbs, spices, or seasonings to gently add flavour.

DRYING
A reduction in the water content of a foodstuff. This is also sometimes referred to as desiccation. This can be done outside in the sun or under cover using a combination of wind and sun, or in special drying rooms or drying machines.

SMOKING
The production and application of smoke to food in a confined space to add flavour and/or act as a preservative. There are two types of smoking: hot and cold. Hot smoking is a cooking process in the presence of smoke to add flavour. Cold smoking is a process using low temperatures to preserve and add flavour, but not cook. Further cooking may be necessary.

Curing: Preserving with Salt

INTRODUCTION TO PRESERVING WITH SALT

Dry salting and brining are important processes in the making of various cured meats. Understanding how these techniques work and how you can use them to add flavour and texture to your food will open new culinary doors for you.

The use of salt in curing both meat and fish forms a key part of many of the techniques in this book. This chapter acts as a reference for many techniques and processes, so you'll be returning to this part of the book time and time again

Wet and Dry Methods

Salt is applied to meat or fish as a preservative either as a "wet" cure – a method usually known as brining – or in dry form: dry salting, either as a rub or by covering the meat or fish completely with salt. Brining and dry salting are in many ways very different processes. But in both techniques, salt is the common factor. In this section, you will find information on the general principles that apply to both techniques. There is no hard and fast rule whether to dry cure in salt or to cure in brine. It depends on what you are making as to whether

you soak the meat or fish in brine, apply a dry-salt rub, or leave to cure packed in dry salt. For more information on choosing the right curing method, see Dry-Salting or Brining? (page 20).

Dry-Salting and Moisture Loss

The essential action of salt in dry curing is to draw out moisture from the flesh. Without water, most bacteria cannot multiply, keeping the food safe to eat (see also About Botulism, page 30). Meat (and fish) is made up from muscle tissue, consisting of muscle fibres, which are in turn made up of hundreds of millions of individual muscle cells. These cells contain fluid enclosed within semi-permeable walls. When salt is applied to the surface of the meat or fish, the cell tries to balance the levels of salt on each side of the wall by sending moisture through the cell wall to dilute the higher salt level on the areas where the salt was applied.

The fluid exchange can cause a loss of up to 15 per cent of the initial weight of the meat or fish. Checking for visual signs of liquid run-off (fluid accumulation in the container) and measuring weight loss are the most effective ways of confirming curing has taken place during dry curing.

Moisture Loss in Brining

The salt present in a brine solution works in a similar way, but because the salt is in solution, as

Salt is used in combination with preservatives for safety in some of the curing processes described in this book.

the cell shrinks, the spaces between the cells allow the brine to penetrate so that the meat tends to retain more moisture than when you apply the salt in a dry form. This is why hot smoking, which uses high temperatures, is often preceded by brining as a method of curing to retain moisture.

Ingredients such as herbs or citrus zest can be added to enhance the flavour of a dry rub or brine.

Firmer Texture

Another effect of the moisture loss caused by salt in curing fish or meat is to increase the firmness of the flesh. This improvement in density and texture is a key feature of some cured meats like air-dried ham or bresaola. Texture is also a key part of Scottish-style smoked salmon, the success of which depends largely on the firmness and texture of the finished product. This is also true for other salt-cured oily fish such as herring and mackerel.

Altered Oil Balance

A third effect of salting, also related to the loss of moisture, is to increase the proportion of oils in the meat or fish. This shift in oil balance has a marked effect on the flavour of the fish or meat, often creating a wonderful intensity.

HEALTH CONCERNS

Salt has been linked to various health scares and health authorities issue clear guidance on the maximum recommended daily intake of salt. (Current National Health Service dietary guidelines recommend that most adults should consume no more than 6g/1 teaspoon of salt per day, and much less if you are in a high-risk group for heart disease or diabetes). It's important to take into account the salt content of the preserved foods you eat in gauging your overall intake; too much is bad for your health. On the plus side, over the centuries the use of salt may well have prevented much ill health by discouraging the growth of many disease-producing bacteria, and helping keep humankind healthy and nourished.

DRY-SALTING OR BRINING?

These processes are both curing treatments involving the application of salt to the product, but have markedly different effects and very different uses. The appropriate uses of each of these methods are explained here.

The choice of whether to cure in brine or apply dry salt depends entirely on what product you're aiming to produce. The table opposite sets out various different products and the type of cure that is required.

Salting Prior to Smoking

As a general rule if you are looking to hot smoke something, it's likely you'll need to use a moisture-rich brine cure before smoking. Hot-smoked products are usually ready to eat straight from the smoker, as hot smoking is also a cooking process. Brining is used because it maintains the moisture in the meat or fish.

Most cold-smoked foods are prepared for smoking with a dry-salt cure, but this is not a hard and fast rule. Some cold-smoked products are too delicate to have a dry-salt cure as this would remove far too much moisture leaving the finished product inedible.

In Practice

A good example of how this choice is made is a kipper, which is a cold-smoked herring that requires further cooking after smoking. Kippers are thin and if they were dry-cured, would lose far too much water, becoming too dry and inedible. Curing in brine maintains the moisture content. (For more information on kippers, see page 50.) Cold-smoked haddock and cod loin are other examples where curing in brine is advantageous.

Some meats such as country hams can either be cured in brine or with a dry-salt cure. Similarly pastrami (page 42) and salt beef (page 38) can be brined or dry cured. The brining method requires full immersion brine and a larger container so, if space is tight, this may be an issue. It is also much more difficult to move large containers of water in and out of some refrigerators. What's more, I find that dry-curing tends to produce a more intense flavour as well as taking less time.

Mackerel are usually dry cured prior to smoking (see Dry-Salted and Air-Dried Mackerel, page 52).

Products such as turkey or chicken that will be cooked by hot smoking are usually cured in brine (see Hot-Smoked Chicken Portions, page 188).

CHOOSING THE TYPE OF CURE

The following table specifies the usual curing method used for
a selection of common cured, dried, or smoked foods.

FOOD	USUAL CURE
Cold-smoked salmon	Dry-salt cure
Hot-smoked salmon	Brine
Kippers (cold-smoked herring)	Brine
Hot-smoked haddock	Brine
Country-style ham	Brine
Gammon	Brine
Salt beef	Brine/dry-salt cure
Pastrami	Brine/dry-salt cure
Air-dried mackerel	Dry-salt cure
Salt cod	Dry-salt cure
Air-dried duck	Dry-salt cure
Dried lamb	Dry-salt cure
Pancetta	Dry-salt cure
Coppa/capicola	Dry-salt cure
Bacon	Dry-salt cure
Sweet-cure bacon	Dry-salt cure
Hot-smoked trout	Brine
Hot-smoked ribs	Brine/dry-salt cure
Hot-smoked chicken	Brine
Hot-smoked turkey	Brine
Hot-smoked goose	Brine
Hot-smoked duck	Brine
Hot-smoked pheasant	Brine
Hot-smoked rabbit	Brine
Hot-smoked venison	Brine

EQUIPMENT YOU WILL NEED

Brining and curing is something that you can undertake in your own kitchen at home, but to make a success of it you need some simple equipment. The items listed here are the basics you'll need to get you started.

Nonreactive Plates and Dishes

While salt works wonders on our food, it will damage any equipment containing iron, copper, or aluminium. If salt comes into contact with these materials it is likely it will cause corrosion, meaning that the salt will dissolve these items over time. The important thing to remember is to avoid any of this corrosion getting into the food. It's far better to use high-grade stainless steel, glass, or plastic containers that won't react with salt, affecting the flavour of the brine, and therefore that of your finished food.

Brining Bucket

A large container made from food-safe, nonreactive material (usually plastic) is necessary if you want to do immersion brining. The size of container you need is dictated by the size of the meat or fish.

Nonreactive Utensils

You'll be doing a lot of stirring to dissolve salt in water when you make your brine. Like the containers you'll be using, you'll need spoons and other utensils made of a material such as plastic that won't react with salt.

Nonreactive Measuring Jug

You will need a large measuring jug made from plastic or high-grade stainless steel for measuring out fluids and other liquid ingredients.

Scales

Kitchen scales are essential for weighing ingredients for your dry cure or brine. Some of the curing salts used in the recipes require accurate measurement

CLEAN IT

Using salt and handling meat and fish can cause problems if you don't keep things clean and tidy. Make sure all your equipment is washed and dried thoroughly after use. If you have used metal equipment that has come into contact with salt, pay particular attention to washing any salt residue from these with hot soapy water.

and having the right set of scales for the job is helpful. I have two sets of scales. One is accurate for small quantities and the other set is for the larger items up to about 6 kg (15 lb). Being able to measure your meat or fish accurately will help you calculate the quantities of ingredients you will

MEASUREMENTS IN THIS BOOK

Measurements in the book are provided for both Imperial and metric scales. Please consistently follow one set of measurements, and do not switch between grams and ounces, for example, when measuring out ingredients. As a general rule of thumb, the smaller the size of the ingredient, the more accurate your scales and measuring need to be. For measuring salts and powders, you need to use very accurate scales or measuring spoons.

KEY

1 Grater
2 Garlic press
3 Nonreactive dishes
4 Pestle and mortar
5 Scales
6 Nonreactive measuring jugs
7 Labels and pen
8 Nonreactive utensils
9 Sharp knife
10 Measuring spoons

IS IT HIGH GRADE?

Although most metal utensils should not be used in contact with curing mixes or brine, high-grade stainless steel is the exception. One way of checking that your utensils are made of high-grade stainless steel is to test with a magnet. High-grade stainless steel is not magnetic. Poorer grades are magnetic and shouldn't be used for curing or brining.

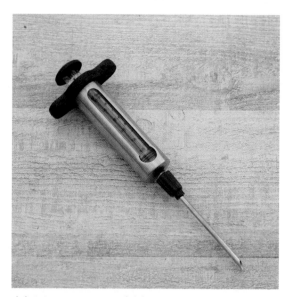

A brining pump is useful for curing thick cuts of meat.

need. Scales are also essential for weighing meat or fish before and after drying to determine if the process is complete. Measuring spoons can be used for small quantities.

Labels

Labels are really useful to record details of the curing time and date information. They can also be used to record the type of product and its weight before curing so that you can compare its weight when the curing is finished.

Brining Pump

This is simply a syringe that is used to inject the meat with brine. You can use a brining pump to inject brine into thicker cuts of meat that would otherwise take too long to cure. This can reduce the overall curing time by as much as 50–60 per cent. A good brining pump is one that has a sturdy construction with as few parts as possible. I use one that is made of polycarbonate and stainless steel. It has a plunger that sits inside the main body and two detachable needles. Look out for one that is food safe and very strong.

Salometer

This is a device that gauges the amount of salt in brine. The salometer floats in the brine and, because liquids with a high salt content have a higher density than weaker solutions, the saltier the

solution, the higher the salometer floats. The salometer has a scale on its main stem and this registers where the scale intersects with the level of the brine. This type of device is very accurate in determining brine strength providing the brine temperature is constant.

INGREDIENTS FOR DRY-SALTING AND BRINES

Your larder is likely to contain a wealth of ingredients that can be added to brines and to make rubs for dry curing. Sweeteners, spices, herbs, vinegars, and lots of other ingredients can be used to create unique and unforgettable flavours in your cured foods.

Salts

There are many different kinds of salt to use for making brines and dry rubs and they each have different characteristics.

Kosher salt This is a light salt for a given volume because of the shape of the individual crystals. The crystals have sharp edges and are particularly suited to making rubs and bacon cures. You can substitute table salt, but you may need to rub it in for longer.

Sea salt Available in large crystal form or in flakes. The large crystals can be used for dry-salting salmon when making cold-smoked salmon. Sea salt flakes are generally used for seasoning finished food. Sea salt is quite expensive and therefore it is not recommended for making brines.

PDV salt Pure dried vacuum salt (PDV) is widely available in large bags. Used for making brines and for dry salting, this salt is cheap and effective. It can also be used as a replacement for regular table salt.

MEASURING SALT

The large crystal size of kosher or sea salt means that a spoonful doesn't weigh the same as a spoonful of fine-grain salts and therefore using volume measurements may not be accurate. My advice is to use scales to weigh the salt for making brine or dry-salt rubs.

Preservatives

In addition to salt, chemical preservatives, principally nitrates and nitrites, often form part of the curing mix, particularly of meat. They are known as bacon cures, nitrite salt cures, cover brines, or cover pickles. The curing salts known as Prague Powders #1 and #2 are proprietary products (see Resources, page 218, for suppliers) containing a mix of common salt and sodium nitrite and/or sodium nitrate. Nitrates (NO_3) either as sodium nitrate ($NaNO_3$) or potassium nitrate or saltpetre (KNO_3), work to prevent the growth of the bacterium *Clostridium botulinum* (see About Botulism, page 30). These preservatives also fix the colour of the meat so that it retains an attractive dark red coloration. For more information on the action of nitrates, see page 26.

Nitrates and nitrites also react with meat to form another group of compounds known as nitrosamines, many of which are potentially carcinogenic (cancer-inducing). Nitrosamines also tend to form in acidic environments as in fermented sausage and when cured meats are cooked at very high temperatures. Products like bacon have the potential to contain high levels of these compounds. For this reason, the permitted levels of nitrates and nitrites in commercial products are strictly controlled. The amounts of these additives specified in the recipes in this book are well within the safety guidelines. Be sure never to exceed the recommended amounts.

WHAT ARE NITRATES AND NITRITES?

These chemicals are primarily used to protect meat from bacterial growth. Nitrites are particularly effective against *Clostridium botulinum*, the bacteria that produce toxins that cause botulism, a potentially fatal condition. Nitrates and nitrites are useful in curing because the processes often demand that meat is kept for long periods at ambient temperatures. These chemicals provide long-term protection for cured meat products. As the nitrate salt naturally oxidizes, the compound loses an oxygen atom and becomes a nitrite (NO_2) compound. These compounds are highly effective in preventing botulism from forming: botulism cannot grow in oxygen-rich environments.

Governments throughout the world legislate on permitted levels of these chemicals to limit the potential health risks from the use of nitrates and nitrites while maintaining microbiological safety. The brining solutions and dry-cure mixes in this book specify concentrations that are well within such legal limits, but it is important to adhere to the amounts specified in the recipes.

Prague Powder #1 This is a blend of salt which contains 6.25 per cent sodium nitrite and 93.75 per cent common salt. This blend is used mainly for brining hams or for any cured meat that will be cooked at a later stage.

Prague Powder #2 This is a blend of salts comprising 6.25 per cent sodium nitrite, 4 per cent potassium nitrate and 89.75 per cent common salt. This blend is used for cured meat that is to be cured and air dried over a long period. The potassium nitrate in this mix converts over time to potassium nitrite, which provides the extended antibacterial action that is needed when curing takes place over a long period.

TYPES OF FLAVOURING

The table below categorizes some of the ingredients you can use to flavour your brines and dry-cure mixes.

HERBS AND SPICES
Rosemary ✚
Thyme
Sage
Juniper ✚
Bay leaf
Coriander
Star anise
Cloves
Cinnamon
Cumin
Chili powder ✿ ★
Paprika ✿ ★
Parsley
Basil
Marjoram
Cayenne pepper ★
Ginger (ground or fresh) ★
Black pepper ★
Garlic powder
Onion powder
Mustard seeds ★
Mustard powder ★
Fennel seeds
Caraway seeds
Mint (dried or fresh)
Oregano

SWEETENERS
Sugar
Treacle ✿
Fructose
Honey
Maple syrup

FRUITS
Citrus juice ♦
Citrus zest ♦

ALCOHOLS
Ale and beer
Cider ♦
Wine ♦
Spirits
Saki

VINEGARS AND SAUCES
White and red wine vinegar ♦
Cider vinegar ♦
Malt vinegar ♦
Worcestershire sauce ♦ ★
Soy sauce (dark and light) ♦
Rice wine vinegar ♦

KEY
These symbols highlight particularly strong qualities:

✿ Adds colour
♦ Adds acidity
★ Adds heat
✚ Aromatic (pungent smell)

BRINING AND DRY-SALTING TIMES FOR MEAT AND FISH

Timing is key to many aspects of successful preserving with salt. Because much depends on the specific type of meat or fish and the size of the piece you are handling, the times given on these pages are for general guidance only. Follow the suggested timings for specific foods elsewhere in this book.

Brine Strength and Timing

Successful brining depends on knowing the strength required of your brine solution. When you know the strength of brine you can track the brining times as a base guide for future brining. Some palettes are not as salt-tolerant as others, so one person may find a food well-seasoned while another may find it too salty. Timings for brining within certain parameters will be a matter of taste. The brine solution table on page 28 shows the proportions of salt and water for different strengths of brine.

Guidelines for Dry-Salting

The timings for dry-salting are dependent on the thickness of the cut as well as the type of fish or meat. When applying salt to the extremities of a cut of meat or fish, bear in mind that areas that are thinner than average will require less salt to cure effectively.

Red meat takes longer to cure than fish as it has tighter muscle fibres and is denser than fish, making it harder for the salt to penetrate the flesh. Curing times vary with different kinds of meats, and the thickness of the cut. What's more, different types of salt will produce slightly different curing times and there will be variations if the salt is mixed with sweeteners and other liquid ingredients. Follow the guidance on timings given for specific products later in this book.

Fish Specifics

The procedures for making products such as Scottish-style cold-smoked salmon all start with a dry-salting process, which draws out moisture from the flesh to improve texture and enrich the flavours. The approximate timings are set out in the table below. The timings do not apply to salt cod or similarly heavily salted products.

The timings in the table assume the use of PDV salt (see page 25). If you are using a coarser salt you may need to adjust the cure time accordingly: Larger crystals of salt will take longer to break down and therefore need longer to cure.

DRY-SALTING TIMES FOR FISH

This table provides broad guidelines for salting fish. The amount of salt used to cover the fish is graded as follows:

Light – a dusting less than 1 mm thick
Medium – a layer 1–2 mm thick
Thick – a covering 2–3 mm thick

FISH FILLET THICKNESS	AMOUNT OF SALT	CURE TIME	DRYING/ RESTING TIME
Thick (50 mm/ 2 in)	Thick	8 hours	36 hours
Medium (25 mm/1 in)	Medium	4 hours	24 hours
Thin (13 mm/½ in)	Light	2 hours	18 hours

BRINE SOLUTIONS

Adhere to a single system of measurement for accuracy when making up your brine.

BRINE STRENGTH	% SALT IN SOLUTION (SAL scale)	WEIGHT OF SALT PER (VOLUME) OF WATER	
		(grams per litre)	(lb/oz per US gallon)
Weak	10	27	3½ oz
	20	55	7½ oz
	30	86	12 oz
	40	118	15 oz
Medium	50	152	1 lb 4 oz
	55	170	1 lb 6 oz
	60	188	1 lb 7 oz
	70	226	1 lb 14 oz
Heavy	80	267	2 lb 3 oz
	90	311	2 lb 9 oz
	100	358	2 lb 15 oz

BRINING TIPS

• Fish is quick to brine; whole-muscle cuts of meat tend to take much longer to brine fully.

• A weak brine usually requires a longer brining time than a strong one.

• Brining for flavour with weaker brines does not preserve the meat and is simply a way of introducing additional flavours.

• Equalize the distribution of salt in the meat or fish after brining by allowing it to rest in the refrigerator before cooking or smoking it.

Herring is brined and then dried before being smoked to make kippers.

BRINING TIMES GUIDELINES

Most types of fish and seafood can be brined for less than an hour, but salt takes much longer to penetrate meat or poultry to any significant depth. You'll need to allow enough time for salt concentrations to equalize throughout. The timings are for raw products, and all should be rinsed in cold water after brining.

PRODUCT	BRINING TIME	BRINE STRENGTH (SAL SCALE)
Prawns	15–20 minutes	60%
Scallops	10–15 minutes	60%
White fish (cod, haddock, etc.)	10–15 minutes	80%
Oily fish (herring, salmon, etc.)	20–25 minutes	80%
Chicken (whole 2–3 kg/4½–6½ lb)	2–2½ hours	80%
Chicken (pieces)	30–40 minutes	80%
Turkey (whole 5–6 kg/11–13 lb)	4–5 hours	80%
Pork belly (skin on)	4–5 hours	60%
Pork ribs (inner membrane removed)	1–2 hours	60%
Pork tenderloin	10–12 hours	25%
Pork chops (25–35 mm/1–1¼ in thick)	1–2 hours	60%
Beef (roasting cut)	12–24 hours	25%

Weakening the brine strength by 10 per cent will allow you to increase the brining time by the same amount. This can be useful if you want to add other flavours and allow them to permeate into the meat without over salting.

SAFETY AND HYGIENE

It is essential with any food preparation to be sure that what you are producing is safe to eat. Curing and brining are techniques that are intended to prevent food spoilage, but you need to observe some sensible precautions in order to ensure that there is no risk of contamination.

One of the primary aims of food preservation is to reduce the possibility of illness resulting from unwanted bacterial infection of food. Salt provides a hostile environment for the vast majority of bacteria and eliminates the risk posed by most of these germs on the food itself. But there is always a risk of cross contamination and spreading germs in the kitchen: a high standard of kitchen cleanliness and personal hygiene is essential. Bacteria – including *Escherichia coli* (*E. Coli*), *Salmonella*, *Listeria monocytogenes*, and *Clostridium botulinum* (see About Botulism, below) – can be spread by poor hygiene practices such as failure to clean kitchen counter surfaces between processes.

ABOUT BOTULISM

Clostridium botulinum (*C. botulinum*) is the bacterium that produces the botulism toxin *C. botulinum* is naturally found in the environment and is present in soil. The bacteria itself isn't dangerous but the toxin it produces can have serious – potentially fatal – consequences. *C. botulinum* doesn't like high levels of salt or acidity and can be controlled by maintaining a clean food-handling environment and good refrigeration (below 3°C/38°F). It thrives without oxygen, so it is less common in whole-muscle cured meats where only surface contamination is likely. It can also be killed through cooking. Nitrates and nitrites are often added to cured products to combat the dangers presented by *C. botulinum*.

Personal Hygiene

Make sure it is second nature to wash your hands before and after handling and preparing food, and after breaks. It is also important to wear the appropriate clothing during food preparation to protect both you and the food from cross contamination. Enforce a no-smoking rule in all food preparation areas.

Surfaces and Equipment

All food preparation surfaces, including chopping boards, should be washed after each food preparation process with anti-bacterial disinfectant or bleach and rinsed with clean water before drying. Similarly, all utensils, containers, and other equipment should be thoroughly washed in hot, soapy water, rinsed, and dried after each use.

Be sure to clean all surfaces after each stage of food preparation.

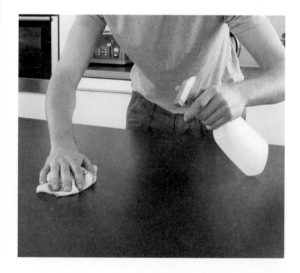

Separation

Keep raw and cured foods well separated in the refrigerator. Keep separate chopping boards for raw and cured or cooked meat and fish.

Don't Wash Raw Meat

There is no need to rinse or wash raw meat unless it is heavily covered with blood or has visible dirt on its surface. Washing raw meat is completely superfluous if you are going on to brine it and has no benefit. There is also danger that washing meat in your kitchen could cause germs to be splashed onto surrounding surfaces, which presents a danger of cross contamination.

Cooking

Cooking is generally accepted as a good method for killing bacteria. Provided the internal temperature of the food reaches a sufficiently high level (at least 74°C/165°F for two minutes), the food will be safe to eat. When hot smoking cured meats, it's likely these temperatures will be achieved, but it's always worth checking the temperature with a meat thermometer to confirm this.

SAFETY SUMMARY

Be sure to follow these simple food safety rules:

• Prevent cooked food and work surfaces from becoming contaminated with raw ingredients.

• Ensure personal hygiene steps are rigorously followed and maintained.

• Ensure raw ingredients are kept at a low temperature and stored appropriately.

• Ensure cooked food is heated to a safe temperature.

Chilling

It is very important to maintain a sufficiently low temperature when preparing brine. It's possible to use ice when making brines to ensure the temperature of the finished solution is low. However, some further chilling is usually required to reduce the temperature of the brine to the ideal temperature of below 5°C (41°F).

Add ice in place of water to brine to bring down the temperature.

FREEZING FISH

Fish caught in the wild can contain parasites, such as Anisakis, that can sometimes survive low-salt brining and smoking at low temperatures. These parasites can be destroyed by cooking at temperatures above 60°C (140°F). You can also make the fish safe to eat raw by freezing at a temperature of -20°C (-4°F) or below for seven days, or if you have a freezer that goes as low as -35°C (-31°F), you can make the fish safe to eat by freezing for just five hours. Fish caught for the preparation of sushi is usually treated in this way – some chefs suggest that freezing improves the texture of the fish too.

BONING AND TYING A HAM

Some ham products are best made with the bone removed and the ham tied with string to retain its shape. Here's how to do it.

Boning

1 Using a sharp (boning) knife and working on the inside of the leg, make an incision between the two muscle joints along the bone. Open this up with your fingers splitting the two muscles as far as possible.

2 Use the knife to separate the meat from both sides of the bone, working the knife underneath the bone to release it. Work slowly to achieve this and remove the bone when all the connective tissue is separated from it. Using the same knife, remove some of the sinew and fat from the inside of the joint. With the joint splayed out on the chopping board, reform the joint by turning it over so the skin side is uppermost.

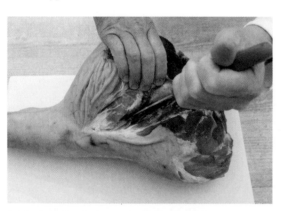

Make an incision between the muscles.

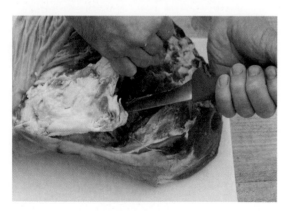

Separate the meat from the bone.

Tying

1 Using butcher's string, tie an initial butcher's knot (page 68) roughly in the middle of the joint to hold it together.

2 Spacing the knots about 50 mm (2 in) apart, tie two more knots either side of the centre knot and repeat the process until you have five knots roughly evenly spaced around the joint. The ham is now ready for brining.

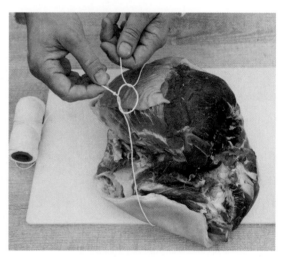

Roll and tie the meat.

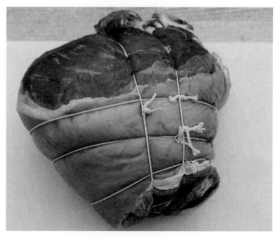

Secure the meat with five knots.

BRINING: COUNTRY-STYLE HAM

33

KEY STAGES
1 Boning and tying (optional)
2 Preparation
3 Brining
4 Cooking

The technique for making this product includes many of the basic brining processes used for foods described later in this book. This tasty ham uses a brining process that allows the meat to develop a sweeter, less salty flavour than a dry cure.

This form of brined ham is also known as Wiltshire ham, named after the English county that throughout the 19th century was renowned as the centre for bacon and ham production in England. This method was devised by John Harris, a village butcher who set up a business wet-curing hams and bacons for the London market. The Harris family embraced the latest innovations, being one of the first curing houses in Britain to use ice to control temperature. Using this technique, they were able to reduce the amount of salt in the cure, producing a sweeter flavour. It was this lighter, sweeter cure that was used for the country-style ham that is so popular in many countries today.

On or Off the Bone?
You will need to decide whether to cure on the bone or off the bone. Some argue that curing off the bone is less traditional, but it does offer some distinct advantages. Curing off the bone makes slicing a little easier when the ham is done and one can achieve impressively large, "dinner-plate sized" slices of ham. It's also possible when curing off the bone to introduce salt and cure into the centre of

Boned country-style ham can be served in impressive dinner-plate size slices.

the meat at the outset, giving potentially a quicker, more even cure. One slight disadvantage of taking the meat off the bone is that it has a tendency to loose its shape. A modern aid to overcome this issue is butcher's netting, elasticated "stocking". which can hold boneless cuts in good shape during curing. If this is not available, you can use several turns of butcher's string to hold the meat in shape. The instructions on the following page assume that you will be preparing the ham off the bone.

Making the Brine

Curing large pieces of pork leg meat to produce ham is quite a simple process: create the brine, immerse the pork and wait a while, boil and or roast the meat – and the end-result is a delicious ham. And the technique is perfectly suited for the home curer if you follow some straightforward steps.

The brine solution is in its simplest form a mixture of water, salt and other seasonings, herbs, spices, and sweeteners. The use of nitrite salts in curing is covered on pages 25–26, and these curing salts may need to be added to the brine to assist with

A whole ham is often easier to handle if it is boned before brining.

preservation, flavour and finished colour. There are significant differences in the rate of nitrite use in brines when compared to dry cures that is vitally important. Follow the specific advice on the use of additional preservatives given for each product.

Preparing the Brine

To work out how much brine to make, simply place the meat in the brining tub and fill it with water. Remove the meat and measure the water. Using the calculations for an 80 per cent brine on page 28 add the required amount of salt. Sometimes it can be useful to use hot water to assist in dissolving the salt but if you do this, you will need to allow the brine to cool before it can be used. Alternatively, make the brine up with 500 ml (1 pint) less water and when the salt is dissolved, add about 450 g (1 lb) of ice cubes to the brine, this will bring the temperature down significantly quicker than if it is left to cool naturally. Don't use the brine until the temperature of the liquid is below 5°C (41°F). Whether or not you add ice, it's likely that you'll have to refrigerate the brine before you use it.

Achieving an Even Cure

To achieve an even cure without having to leave the meat in the brine for up to a month, you can inject some brine into the thickest parts of the muscle. This will speed up the curing process and prevent partial curing. This occurs when the inner parts of the thickest muscle are not exposed to the brine and therefore remain uncured. The uncured meat doesn't take on the colour of cured ham leaving parts of the finished ham grey in the middle, which can spoil the effect.

Injecting brine is done by simply probing the pork joint with a syringe-like brine pump (see page 24). Measure the brine that you inject to make sure that you increase the weight of the joint by no more than 10 per cent. Aim for the thickest parts of the muscle first and work a pattern around the joint, paying particular attention to the parts of the muscle directly underneath the fat cap.

Brining a Ham

1 Put the ham into the container you intend to use for brining and add enough water to cover it. Measure the amount of water used to indicate how much brining solution you will need. Prepare and cool the brine by adding ice as described on page 31.

2 Put the ham back into the brining container and pour over the brine. The ham will have a tendency to float on the surface of the salted water. To get around this problem, place a weight such as a small plate on top of the ham. This should be sufficient weight to keep the meat submerged. Try to avoid trapping any air pockets under the saucer when placing it on top of the joint. Cover the container and check every day.

3 The length of time the meat needs to stay in the brine depends upon its size. A simple method is to measure the thickness of the meat and allow three days per 25 mm (1 in), measured from the edge to the middle of the meat, plus an additional two days. If the ham is large, you may need to consider injecting brine into the thickest parts of the meat (see facing page). Keep the ham in the refrigerator for the allotted time, turning it every couple of days to ensure that the meat cures evenly on all sides.

Cooking and Serving

The brined ham should be boiled in fresh water and then roasted for long enough for the internal temperature of the meat to reach 71°C (160°F). This should be checked with a meat thermometer. The ham can be served hot or cold.

YOU WILL NEED

- **4.5–5 kg (10–11 lb) pork leg joint (aitch bone and hock removed)**

FOR 6 LITRES (12½ PINTS) OF BRINE

- **5 litres (10½ pints) water**
- **1 kg (2¼ lb) ice**
- **1.4 kg (3 lb) salt**
- **100 g (3½ oz) Prague Powder #1**
- **4 star anise (crushed)**
- **2 cinnamon sticks (crushed)**
- **5 bay leaves (crushed)**
- **2 tbsp. black peppercorns (cracked)**
- **20 juniper berries (crushed)**
- **5 tbsp. white wine vinegar**

Add ice to the prepared brine.

Immerse the ham in the brine.

GAMMON

Gammon is a brined and cold-smoked cut of pork taken from the thigh or the rump of the pig. Gammon can be prepared with the bone in or more commonly, boned and tied. It is usually roasted prior to serving.

KEY STAGES

1 Boning

2 Brining

3 Rinsing

4 Drying

5 Cold smoking

The technique for curing gammon is similar to that used for brining country-style ham. The difference for me is in the recipe for the cure. I normally use a salt and brown sugar cure for gammon to produce a classic flavour – I also add a little crushed juniper into the mix to add an "extra something" to the overall effect. If you want to add more flavours to gammon, it's best do this when you roast it.

You will need to remove the femur bone and reform the leg back after curing and smoking. The easiest way to do this before curing is to use butcher's netting or meat net, which is like an open-mesh support bandage covering the complete leg. Reform the meat and insert it into a tube, enclosed in the netting. Push the meat through the tube so that it emerges surrounded by the netting. A more traditional way of presenting the boned gammon is to tie it back into a joint using butcher's string (see page 32).

Roasted gammon is a flavourful focus for a hot main course or a cold buffet.

TIP

If you don't have a container that's big enough to cure the gammon in, you can use a strong food bag to enclose the meat and brine.

YOU WILL NEED
- **4.5–5 kg (10–11 lb) pork thigh (aitch bone and hock removed)**

FOR THE BRINE
- **4.5 litres (8 pints) water**
- **750 g (1 lb 10 oz) salt**
- **200 g (7 oz) brown sugar**
- **25 g (1 oz) juniper berries (crushed)**
- **50 g (2 oz) Prague Powder #1**

1 Heat the water in a stainless steel vessel until it is just beginning to boil and turn off the heat. Add the dry ingredients and stir until the sugar and salt are fully dissolved. Allow the brine to cool to room temperature and then refrigerate until its temperature is 3–5°C (37–41°F).

2 Place the ham in the brine and allow it to cure for three days per inch of thickness in the refrigerator. Ensure that the ham is fully immersed. If necessary, place a plate on top of the meat to help to keep it submerged. Turn the meat daily if you're not sure it is fully immersed.

3 After it has cured, remove the meat from the brine and rinse it under cold running water. Dry the meat and place it on a rack in the refrigerator to air dry for a further two days.

4 The gammon can now be cold smoked for 24–28 hours depending on your taste. Use oak, apple, cherry, or beech for the best results. (For full instructions on smoking, see pages 132–157.)

Rinse the cured meat under cold running water.

COOKING AND SERVING

For best results cook the gammon in a roasting bag in the oven until the internal temperature of the meat reaches 71°C (160°F). Leave the gammon to cool naturally and then refrigerate.

Remove the gammon from the roasting bag and discard any cooking juice as this will contain quite a lot of salt. With a sharp knife, remove the strings holding the joint in place. Using your fingers and working slowly, part the skin from the fat leaving the fat intact on the meat. When the whole skin has been removed, the gammon is ready to slice and serve.

SALT BEEF

Salt beef is popular in many cultures around the world and it's no wonder why. This cured beef delicacy is made from brisket, which is one of the most underrated cuts of meat on the market.

Brisket is one of those cuts of meat that requires some investment in time before it can be enjoyed. On it's own it can be tough, but when it's been cured for a week in brine and then cooked gently for three hours with some stock vegetables you have a wonderfully delicate and tasty dish that you'll want to make over and over again. Brisket is marbled with sinew and has lovely layers of fat, which add flavour to the finished salt beef. Although the technique I use here is a brine cure, it is possible to create a similar result by dry curing in a bag using a similar technique to that described for pastrami (see page 42).

Salt beef is a delicious sandwich filler – often served with rye bread and pickles. It can also be eaten as a main course with potatoes and vegetables.

Add the brine ingredients to warm water.

YOU WILL NEED

- **2.5 kg (5½ lb) beef brisket**

FOR THE BRINE
- **4 litres (7 pints) water**
- **750 g (1 lb 10 oz) salt**
- **4 cloves of garlic (bruised)**
- **1 tbsp. thyme**
- **5 bay leaves**
- **1 tsp. cracked black pepper**
- **1 star anise (crushed)**
- **3 cloves (crushed)**
- **5 tsp. Prague Powder #1**

Trim visible fat from the meat.

Brining the Meat

1 Fill a stainless steel cooking vessel with the water. Warm the water and before it boils remove from the heat. Add all the brine ingredients to the water and stir until all the salt has dissolved. Allow the brine to cool and then place in the refrigerator to chill to 3–5°C (37–41°F).

2 While the brine is cooling, place the brisket on a chopping board. Trim away any particularly large pieces of fat leaving a maximum of 10 mm (½ in) thickness of fat. Pierce the surface of the brisket at 25-mm (1 in) intervals with a knife. This will allow the brine to penetrate more easily – advisable where the meat is covered with a layer of fat. Immerse the meat in the brine and cure in the refrigerator for one week. Turn every day to ensure an even cure.

Place the meat in the brine and cure for a week.

FOR THE COOKING STOCK
- **2 onions**
- **2 carrots**
- **2 celery sticks**
- **3 cloves of garlic**
- **Sprig of thyme**
- **2 bay leaves**
- **Sage leaves**

Cooking and Serving

1 Remove the brisket from the brine and place it in the cooking vessel. Soak it in cold fresh water for eight hours. Drain the water and refill to cover the meat by 5 cm (2 in). Roughly chop the onions, carrots and celery. Add the lightly crushed cloves of garlic to the pot and then add the thyme, bay leaves, and a few sage leaves. Bring to the boil and reduce the heat to simmer gently for two hours.

While still in the pot, cover the meat with a piece of baking parchment and allow to cool naturally. When the brisket has cooled enough to handle, remove it from the pot.

2 Slice the salt beef across the grain with a sharp knife. Serve piping hot with boiled vegetables or use in a cold meat sandwich on rye bread, traditionally served with lashings of sauerkraut and pickled chillis or dill pickles and horseradish.

The cooked salt beef is drained and sliced. It can be served hot or cold.

Cover the meat with water and add vegetables.

Cover with baking parchment and cool.

Salt Beef Hash

Perfect for a quick and easy meal, this is one of those satisfying heart-warming dishes you and your family will appreciate on a cold day.

INGREDIENTS

- 450 g (1 lb) cooked salt beef
- 500 g (1¼ lb) new potatoes
- 1 large onion (roughly chopped)
- 1 clove of garlic
- 2 tbsp. olive oil or butter
- 2 tbsp. Worcestershire sauce
- 2 tbsp. tomato purée
- Salt and pepper to taste

Serves 4

METHOD

1 Boil the new potatoes in a pan of salted water for 10–12 minutes. Meanwhile, prepare the cooked salt beef by cutting it into thin slices across the grain and into small pieces.

2 Fry the onion and garlic in a hot pan with the olive oil or butter for a couple of minutes until the garlic cooks through and the onions become translucent. Remove the onions and set aside.

3 Drain the potatoes and cut into halves. Add the potatoes to the pan and fry until they begin to turn golden. Add the fried onions, salt beef, tomato purée, and Worcestershire sauce. Reduce the heat and cook through for 5–10 minutes. Gently stir with a spoon to combine. Reduce the heat and cook through for 5–10 minutes. Serve with crusty bread and plenty of butter.

PASTRAMI

Pastrami is a brined and smoked beef brisket, a cut also known as a "flat". Originating in a form of cured meat traditionally made in Romania, it has gained huge popularity as a sandwich meat and has become a classic American food.

This is a really easy cured meat to prepare. Pastrami is first brined with seasonings and then hot smoked with more seasonings. The main flavours associated with pastrami are pepper, coriander, garlic, and paprika. The instructions here are based on a 2.5 kg (5½ lb) brisket, which is a manageable size. Adjust the quantities accordingly if your meat is a different weight.

YOU WILL NEED

- **2.5 kg (5½ lb) beef brisket**

FOR THE CURE
- **250 g (9 oz) salt**
- **3 tsp. Prague Powder #1**
- **50 g (2 oz) sugar (optional)**
- **2 pints (1 litre) chilled water**
- **2 tbsp. ground coriander**
- **2 tbsp. cracked black pepper**
- **2 tsp. smoked paprika**
- **2 tsp. garlic powder**

FOR THE SEASONING
- **2 tbsp. ground coriander**
- **2 tbsp. cracked black pepper**
- **2 tsp. smoked paprika**
- **2 tsp. garlic powder**

Trim the excess fat and sinew.

Preparing and Curing the Meat

1 Trim the excess fat, skin, and sinew from the meat and pat dry. Use a small knife to pierce both the upper and lower surfaces. This will allow the cure to penetrate. Place the meat in a nonreactive dish. Mix together the salt, Prague Powder, sugar, and water, and stir until dissolved.

2 Mix the remaining cure ingredients together and massage into the meat. Pour over the brine, cover, and cure in the refrigerator for seven days. Turn the meat daily.

3 After curing is complete, remove the meat from the brine and rinse under cold running water to remove all traces of the cure. Immerse the meat in sufficient cold water and soak for one hour. Drain and pat dry with kitchen paper.

4 Lay the brisket in a nonreactive tray. Apply the seasoning mix to the surface of the meat to create a herb crust. Use one-third of the mix on the bottom and sides and the remaining two thirds on the top.

Pastrami is served in thin slices cut across the grain of the meat.

Massage the cure into the meat.

Pour over the brine and refrigerate for seven days.

Smoking

You can either hot or cold smoke pastrami. It is important not to overcook pastrami during smoking otherwise the meat will become tough and dry. Low and slow is the key here; low temperatures and a long cooking time will ensure you get the right texture. Brisket can be tough if it is not cooked for long enough or if it's cooked at too high a temperature. Be sure to read the general instructions on hot and cold smoking before tackling this stage (see pages 132–157).

Hot-Smoke Method

Aim to hot smoke the meat for around six hours at 80°C (176°F), aiming for the meat to reach an internal temperature of 72°C (162°F). This can be checked using a meat thermometer. Smoke with oak or a fruit wood such as cherry or apple to impart an aromatic smoky flavour and colour to your pastrami.

Cold-Smoke Method

If you haven't got a hot smoker, you can cook your brisket in the oven before smoking it. Be careful here as even 140°C (284°F) will be too hot. You will be aiming for an internal temperature of 72°C (162°F) in the thickest part of the brisket. To achieve this, aim for an oven temperature slightly higher than your target internal temperature, as there will be a lag in temperature rise for the internal part of the meat. This may sound obvious but it's worth mentioning because in order to achieve the required internal temperature but avoid overcooking the brisket, it is absolutely necessary to take your time cooking this slab of meat so the outside temperature doesn't exceed 80°C (176°F). Once the brisket has cooled it can be placed in a cold smoker for two to four hours (depending on your taste preference).

Pastrami on Rye

Pastrami is a classic sandwich filler. Served on fresh rye bread, this is a New York deli staple. There are many variations on this traditional way of serving pastrami, but here is my favourite.

METHOD

1 Lightly butter two slices of rye bread. Put a generous helping of sliced pastrami on one of the slices.

2 Smear a thin layer of mustard on the meat and top with a thinly sliced dill pickle and it's ready to serve.

PRE-BRINING A WHOLE CHICKEN

Brine serves a key role in preparing chicken for smoking. This step can be applied in a similar way to other meats too. The process also improves the texture and flavour of the meat.

Brine serves an important role in preparing the chicken for hot or cold smoking. And this step can be useful even if you're just roasting the bird in a conventional way and want to give it a special boost. In the cold-smoking process the pre-brining stage helps keep the meat safe from bacteria while smoking is taking place. Unlike dry salting, brining also serves to preserve some of the moisture in the bird when it is cooked or hot smoked.

Preparing the Chicken and the Brine

1 Remove any excess fat or skin from the bird. Using a boning knife, remove the wishbone from the neck end. This can be found sitting just under both breasts at the neck entrance to the bird. I prefer to remove the wishbone because it makes the bird easier to carve when it has been cooked.

2 Place the chicken in the bottom of a nonreactive container large enough to hold the chicken. Measure the amount of water needed to cover the chicken and round this up to the nearest litre (or pint). Remove the chicken from the container, drain it, and place to one side.

3 Add 250 g of salt to every litre of water (4 oz/1 pint). This will make a roughly 80 per cent brine. Stir the brine until all of the salt is dissolved. Add two bay leaves, one teaspoon of cracked black pepper, a sprig of thyme, a crushed garlic clove, and the juice and zest of a lemon. Stir well and allow the brine to chill in the refrigerator. When the brine is chilled, immerse the chicken and allow it to cure for two hours.

4 Remove the chicken from the brine and rinse it inside and out with cold running water. Pat the chicken dry, place on a wire rack and return it to the refrigerator to dry for two hours. The bird is now ready for hot or cold smoking.

Remove the wishbone.

Immerse the chicken in brine for two hours.

Dry the chicken in the refrigerator on a wire rack.

JOINTING A BIRD

Jointing a bird gives you many options. You can freeze individual pieces for later or use the pieces in a variety of ways. Buying a whole bird can be cost-effective, and jointing is easy if you follow these simple steps.

I was taught this easy way of jointing a chicken by a really experienced chef. I won't pretend that this is the only way to joint a bird as there are a number of different ways to do this. But the method I use works well and with a little practice and patience, you should make an excellent job of it. You'll need a large chopping board and a sharp carving knife. This method of jointing will give you six main pieces plus the two wings. If you want to end up with eight portions, simply divide the breasts into two.

Removing the Legs

1 Start with the bird flat on the board, with the breast uppermost. Pull the legs apart slightly and cut into the skin between the legs and the breast exposing the flesh.

2 Bend the leg back to dislocate the hip joint. Cut between the tip of the leg joint and the hip to remove the leg from the carcass. Repeat this step for the other leg.

3 To separate the drumstick from the thigh, work on the inside of the leg. Look for the natural leg joint. It's sometimes easy to see this because there is a line of fat running across the joint. Use your knife to part the thigh and the drumstick.

4 To tidy up the drumstick, make a cut around the drumstick towards the ankle end severing all the tendons. Firmly dislocate the joint from the ankle and remove.

This method produces eight pieces.

Cut into the skin between the legs and the breast.

Separate the drumstick from the thigh.

Removing the Breast

1 To remove the breast, first remove the wishbone, which is located at the neck end. With the back of your knife, rub against the bone to expose it on both sides. Use your finger to pass behind the bone and release it from any breast meat.

2 Make an incision close to the breastbone on one side. Cut along the bone and the rib cage. The meat should come away quite easily. To remove the breast fully from the carcass, dislocate the wing bone from its joint at the neck end. Then cut the breast away from the carcass by cutting through this joint. Repeat this process to remove the remaining breast.

Cut along the breastbone and the rib cage.

Pull the breast meat away from the rib cage.

Removing and Trimming the Wings

1 Find the root of the wing bone and cut it away from the breast ensuring you leave as much meat on the breast as possible.

2 To trim the wings and remove the tips, find the joint between the tip and the middle part of the wing and make a cut in the centre of the joint. There should be little resistance to this cut. To finish off all the joints trim the fat around the meat to remove any straggly bits.

Separate the wing from the breast.

Remove the wing tips.

TIPS

• Chill the chicken before jointing. You'll find the fat will stay on the bird and it will be less slippery to work with if it is very cold.

• Don't discard any of the trimmings or bones as you can use these to make a delicious stock, which can be frozen for future use in soups and casseroles.

BACK CUTTING HERRING FOR KIPPERS

To make an authentic kipper, you'll need to prepare the fish before curing and smoking. This is called back cutting and is not a complicated technique to learn.

When you see kippers in a traditional smoke house they are usually arranged on hooks (tenterhooks) set into wooden poles (spates). The herring sit high up in the roof of the smoker tightly packed together to make best use of the available space. To expose each kipper adequately to the smoke, the fresh herring needs to be flattened out. Traditionally this was done using a process known as back cutting. In modern commercial operations this is now done by machine. But the traditional method works well for home smokers. Essentially the process involves simply gutting the fish through its back rather than cutting through its belly cavity and removing the guts in the usual way.

TIPS

• Take your time with the initial cut and don't press the knife too deeply into the gut cavity.

• Keep the tail intact. Don't continue the cut through the tail.

• Herrings are oily fish and can cause a skin reaction in some people. When handling fish, it's a good idea to wear food preparation gloves, which are widely available in shops or online.

Cutting Along the Back

1 To start the back cut it's worth just taking a moment to consider what it is you are actually trying to achieve. The main objective of this technique is to flatten the fish keeping it in one piece. The first cut is made along the herring's back just to one side of the dorsal fin and backbone from the back of the head towards the tail. To do this, stand the fish up so that its dorsal fin is uppermost. Take care not to cut too deeply and risk cutting the belly and so separating the two sides of the fish. Start by pressing the knife through the ribs into the belly cavity and work towards the tail.

2 Reverse the fish and continue the same cut towards the head, cutting between the eyes and pressing the knife down through the head towards the bottom jaw of the herring. The head is quite tough at this point and a little pressure is needed to penetrate through the bone. Be careful not to cut through the bottom jaw.

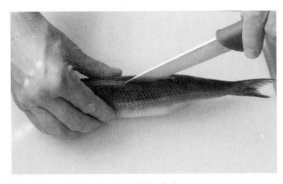

Cut through the back of the fish.

Continue cutting between the eyes.

Cleaning and Flattening

1 When the cut has been made along the length of the fish without going all the way through, open the back cut, remove and discard the guts. Rinse the fish in cold running water to remove any residual blood and lay it skin side down on a chopping board.

2 Using your fingers, remove the gills and discard. If the fish appears not to be lying flat, turn it over so it's facing skin side up and with the heel of your hand press down lightly on the head to make it lay flat. The herring is now ready to be brined (see page 50). If you have not already made the brine, place the fillets on a wire rack and keep refrigerated until the brine is ready.

Open the back of the fish.

Back cutting is the first stage in the kipper-making process.

Remove the gills and discard.

BRINING HERRINGS FOR KIPPERS

I have often said that making your own kippers is a bit of a one-way street. In other words, once you've made this delicacy yourself, there really is no going back to shop-bought products. Simple to make, you can't help but enjoy this traditional cured and cold-smoked herring.

KEY STAGES

1 Preparation

2 Brining

3 Drying

4 Smoking

Kippers are the name given to cold-smoked herrings. They have a distinctive taste and over the years have drifted in and out of fashion. Although commercially produced versions of varying quality are available, in my opinion, there is no doubt that there's nothing that can compare to a kipper that you've lovingly prepared, cured, and smoked yourself. If you've never done this before, the instructions on the following pages will get you started. The essentials of the smoking process are described on pages 132–157.

Choosing Your Fish

North Atlantic herrings are the traditional fish used for making kippers. These fish are widely available in supermarkets or from a good fishmonger. When buying herring, look for freshness in the fish. Check the eyes; they should be dark, not opaque or milky. Also take a look at the gills. As fish begin to deteriorate, their gills become a little brown. Fresh fish tend to have red gills – the redder the better.

Preparing and Curing

Having bought your fish, you'll need to prepare it for curing by back cutting. This is done so the largest possible surface area of the fish is exposed to the cure and the smoke (see page 48).

Once you have back cut the fish, you're ready to cure the fish in the brine solution. The reason for curing in brine rather than using a dry-salt cure is

ON TENTERHOOKS

In commercial smoke houses the kippers are fixed onto small steel pins (tenterhooks) on wooden frames to keep them flat. This traditional system was used as far back as the 14th century.

Kippers are cured with a simple salt and water brine.

simple: because the fish is relatively thin, adding dry salt would reduce the water content of the flesh, making the kipper too dry.

Making the Brine

1 Place the fish in a nonreactive container. Fill with sufficient water to immerse the fish. Remove the fish and measure the water. This is the volume of brine you need. Prepare the brine allowing 250 g of salt for every litre of cold water (4 oz/1 pint). This creates an 80 per cent (SAL scale) solution (see page 28). Stir well and allow the brine to stand until it becomes clear.

Immerse the herring in the brine and weigh down with a plate or dish to ensure the fish is completely submerged. Place the brining container in the refrigerator and leave for 20 minutes to cure.

2 Remove the herring from the brine and rinse under cold, running water. Pat dry and place on a food rack in the refrigerator to dry for about two hours. A slightly sticky salt glaze called a pellicle will develop on the surface of the fish, which helps the smoke to adhere. This resting time in the refrigerator also allows the salt to equalize throughout the fish, a process that continues even while the fish is smoking, and afterwards when it is being stored.

Smoking

After curing and resting, remove the herring from the refrigerator. It is now ready for cold smoking. Full instructions on this stage of the preparation process are given on page 164.

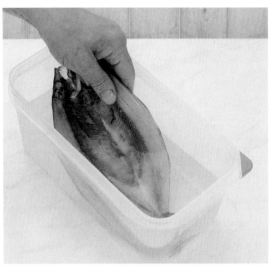

Immerse the herring in the brine.

Place a weight over the fish to keep it submerged.

A SWEETER BRINE

Traditionally kippers are cured with a salt-only brine. Some people find this a little harsh for their taste. You may like to try adding 50 g (2 oz) of sugar per 500 ml (1 pint) of brine. Be aware that this may take a little time to dissolve into the brine solution.

Place the fish on a rack in the refrigerator to rest.

DRY CURING: DRY-SALTED AND AIR-DRIED MACKEREL

Air-dried mackerel is something that tastes out of the ordinary but is simple to prepare in the right conditions. This method of preparation captures the distinctive flavour of this widely available fish, creating a delicacy that is delicious on its own or as the basis for a tasty pâté.

KEY STAGES

1 Cleaning and curing

2 Drying

Mackerel (*Scomber scombrus*) is an oily fish with a stripy skin that roams the oceans in large shoals, allowing these fish to be netted in vast numbers. There are many species of mackerel, but in my opinion air drying works best with Atlantic (or Boston) mackerel. Catching large numbers of fish is only a good thing if you can process them in bulk. Before the days of refrigeration there had to be a reliable way of preserving these large catches. One of the easiest methods was to start the preservation process with salt to cure the fish and to assist in removing excess moisture thus preventing bacterial growth.

Outdoor Method

In warmer climates where there is enough sun, the mackerel can be dried in the open air. Usually this takes place on mats or with the fish suspended on lines. The latter being the preferred method as this allows the passage of air over the entire fish. Mackerel is usually air dried with the head on and the guts removed.

Indoor Method

Not all of us have the benefit of a warm, dry sunny climate to assist us in making this little delicacy, and this needn't be a problem. If you have a dehydrator or a fan oven you can dry mackerel without the need for the right weather conditions.

Making air-dried mackerel is an ideal project to try outside if conditions allow.

Cleaning and Curing

1 First gut and clean the fish, removing the blood line (the darker meat that carried the blood supply) with your finger. Rinse the fish under cold running water and pat dry with kitchen paper. You can remove the gills if you prefer but it's not essential.

2 Sprinkle about 3 mm (¹/₈ inch) of salt in the base of a nonreactive dish and place the whole fish on the salt layer. Fill the gut cavity of the fish with salt and then cover the entire fish with salt. Cover the dish with clingfilm and leave the fish to cure in the refrigerator for three hours.

3 Remove the mackerel from the salt and rinse under cold, running water. Pat dry with kitchen paper, ensuring you rinse and dry the gut cavity too. Weigh the fish as this will help you judge how much moisture has been lost at the end of drying.

Fill the gut cavity with salt.

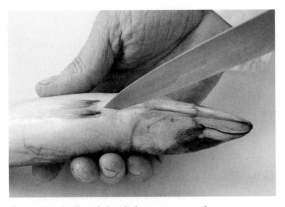

Open the belly of the fish to remove the guts.

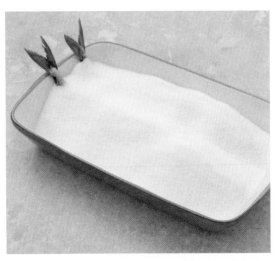

Cover the entire fish with salt.

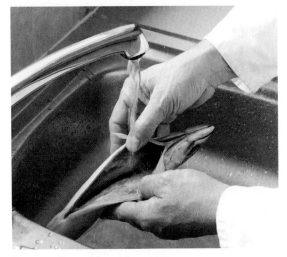

Rinse under cold running water.

After three hours remove the salt.

Drying

1 If your climate is not right for outdoor drying, lay the cured fish on a wire rack with the gut cavity facing downwards and with the belly flaps open. Arrange two fish per wire rack and place them in a fan oven on a very low heat. It is important to set the oven correctly as you don't want to cook the fish. If the temperature is too high the heat will alter the proteins in the fish causing it to lose the delicate texture you're looking for.

Set the oven temperature to between 40°C and 50°C (122–104°F). This is likely to be the lowest temperature setting available on many fan ovens. Leave the door of the oven a little open. This will assist drying. In these conditions, the temperature of the fish will rarely reach 40°C (104°F) and will simulate the drying conditions had the fish been exposed directly to full sun.

2 The fish will be ready when the skin is wrinkled and the feel of the flesh has firmed up to the touch. Mackerel usually contain between 60 and 74 per cent water. So in every kilogram of fish there is between 600–740 millilitres (9–11 fl oz/1 pint) of water. At the end of three hours in the oven drying, remove the fish and weigh it. You're looking for a loss of about 30 per cent compared with its pre-drying weight.

TIPS

• Make sure the wire rack you are using will fit safely inside your oven before you start.

• Many oven doors are spring loaded. You may need to wedge the door open with a metal implement.

• When the mackerel is hung by its tail, the gut cavity naturally closes. To promote drying, hold the gut cavity open using cut down wooden skewers (see picture on page 52).

Open-Air Drying

If you are in a warm climate, you can suspend the mackerel by the tail and peg the fish onto a line outside to dry. For the mackerel to dry effectively, the temperature should be at least 30°C (80°F) with a relative humidity of 50–70 per cent. The other important factor for effective air drying is the presence of a good breeze.

Air-Dried Mackerel Pâté

This pâté is easy to make and simply delicious.

INGREDIENTS
- 1 whole dry-salted and air-dried mackerel
- 4 tbsp. mayonnaise
- 1 tbsp. horseradish sauce
- 1 tsp. cayenne pepper
- Juice of half a lemon
- Small bunch of chives (finely chopped)
- White pepper and salt

To serve:
- Crispbread
- Small sprig of thyme
- 5 cm (2 in) piece of cucumber (sliced)

METHOD

1 Submerge the mackerel in a pan of boiling water (unsalted) and turn off the heat and leave for ten minutes.

2 Separate the flesh in flakes from the skin and bones, and set aside to cool. Fold in the mayonnaise, horseradish, cayenne pepper, chives, and lemon juice, and season to taste with white pepper and salt.

3 Serve on crispbread, garnished with a slice of cucumber and a sprig of thyme.

54

GUTTING AND FILLETING A SALMON

Several techniques in this book specify fillets of salmon. Although many fishmongers will do this for you, knowing how to create bone-free fillets from a whole salmon is a useful skill to add to your armoury.

Salmon is a delicate fish and rough handling will separate the flakes – if you're going to make fillets for curing (see page 62), you'll need to take this into account. If the flakes become separated and you're dry salting the fish, too much salt may enter the gaps between the flakes causing the fish to be overcured in parts.

1 Lay the salmon on its side with its belly towards you. Make a slit along its belly from the vent (anus) to its gills or lug bones. Discard the guts. Use your finger to break the blood line at the back of the gut cavity. Rinse out the cavity under running water.

2 Place the salmon with the dorsal fin towards you. Make a vertical cut behind the gill plates towards the spine and stop when you reach it. Turn the knife so the blade faces down the length of the fillet towards the tail and the knife rests on top of the spine.

3 Make a horizontal cut following the line of the spine towards the tail. Take your time with this and make sure the knife stays level and close to the bone. Cut through the rib bones where they join onto the spine. Continue the cut until you release the fillet. Turn the fish onto the other side and repeat to remove the other fillet.

Filleting a salmon provides two large pieces of boneless fish – perfect for many dishes.

SALMON SAFETY

If you're using a whole salmon, it's likely you'll have bought from a fishmonger or supermarket, unless you're one of the lucky ones who have the opportunity to go salmon fishing. If you have caught your own salmon, you'll need to freeze the fish to -4°F (-20°C) for 24 hours to kill any parasites that may be present. If your freezer doesn't produce such low temperatures, simply extend the freezing time to seven to ten days. Shop-bought salmon will already have been treated in this way before sale.

4 To remove the rib bones, lay the fillet flesh side up on the chopping board. Working from the middle of the fillet, place a filleting knife just under the rib bones and cut towards the belly, angling the knife slightly up to keep the edge just under the ribs. With the rib bones removed, trim the edges of the fillet to remove the belly fat and fin bones. Repeat the process for the other fillet.

5 Use a pair of fish tweezers to remove the small bones that sit just above the spine. Run your finger from the head end of the fillet to feel these bones as you pass over them. Grip each bone with the tweezers and tug lightly to remove them. There are 22 or 23 of these bones, but once you're in a rhythm it takes only a short time. Repeat for the second fillet and now you have two fillets of salmon ready for curing in a variety of ways.

TIPS

• If you have trouble keeping the knife close to the spine when filleting and leave some of the salmon flesh on the bone, use a spoon to remove the remaining flesh and freeze it for future use in making a salmon mousse, for example.

• You can make it easier to remove the rib bones by placing a rolled up cloth under the belly flap to straighten it a little.

Make the first cut behind the gills.

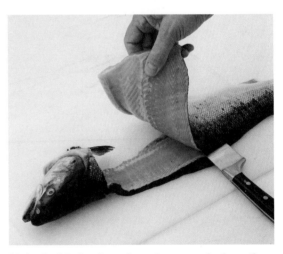

Slide the blade along the spine towards the tail.

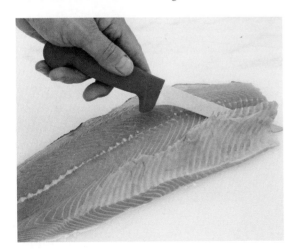

Remove the rib bones.

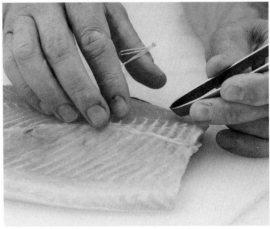

Use tweezers to remove any small bones.

GRAVLAX DRY-CURED SALMON

Gravlax is the name given to Scandinavian-style dry-cured salmon, which means literally "grave salmon". This is because traditionally it was made by burying the fish on the shoreline below the water level. This exquisite dish is really easy to make.

KEY STAGES

1 Preparation

2 Curing

3 Marinating

In the past to make gravlax (or gravad lax) fishermen would bury their salmon in the sand on the shore until it had fermented. Fermentation is no longer used in the making of this dish. Today it is prepared by dry curing fillets of salmon in salt and sugar, with the addition of dill. The salmon is usually layered in a dish under a weight to increase moisture loss, and it is cured in the refrigerator.

A variety of other strong flavours and aromatics are often added in the preparation of this delicacy as well as the use of ingredients such as beetroot, to add colour, or horseradish, which adds a kick.

To prepare gravlax you need two sides of salmon, filleted and pin boned with the skin on. (See page 56, for instructions on how to fillet a salmon.) It is possible to make gravlax using skinless salmon, but I prefer it with the skin on as it makes handling and carving so much easier. It's also less likely that you'll damage the fish if the skin is still in place. Removing the skin after it is cured is a simple process.

The following technique and measurements are suitable for two sides of salmon, skin on, filleted, and pin boned.

Gravlax garnished with chooped beetroot, lemon, capers, and a sprinkling of fresh dill is a perfect starter or light lunch snack.

Preparing and Curing

1 Take a nonreactive tray large enough to lay both salmon fillets next to each other. Lay a sheet of clingfilm over the base. There should be enough clingfilm to enclose the fish.

2 Sprinkle a thin layer of salt evenly across the lined base of the tray. Place the first fillet skin side down on one side of tray. Lay the second salmon fillet next to the first fillet so they are just touching. Ensure the head and tail ends are lying in the same direction (head to head, tail to tail).

3 Mix the salt and sugar together and sprinkle onto the fillets, ensuring you coat the fish evenly. Sprinkle the ground black pepper evenly across the two fillets then cover evenly with half the dill. Drizzle the vodka (if using) over both fillets.

4 Place one fillet over the other to create a "sandwich". Wrap the clingfilm tightly around the salmon and secure it into a firm package. Use additional clingfilm if required.

5 Place the wrapped salmon fillets in a nonreactive dish and place a weight such as a flat dish with a jug of water on top. Put this in the refrigerator and cure for three days turning the package every 12 hours.

YOU WILL NEED
- Two 1–2 kg (1¼–2½ lb) sides of salmon (filleted and boned, skin on)

FOR THE BASIC CURE
- 50 g (2 oz) salt
- 30 g (1 oz) brown sugar
- 1 tsp. ground black pepper
- 1 tbsp. vodka (optional)
- 1 bunch dill

FOR THE MARINADE AND GARNISH
- 1 beetroot
- 25 mm (1 in) horseradish root (peeled and grated)
- Olive oil

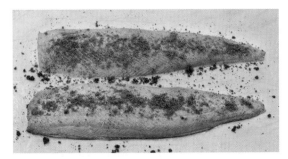

Sprinkle the cure mixture onto the salmon fillets.

Cover with dill and drizzle with vodka (if used).

Place a weight on top of the wrapped salmon.

Marinating and Serving

1 When the salmon is cured, remove it from the refrigerator and lightly rinse off the remaining salt/sugar cure with cold running water. Do not rub the salmon at this stage or you will lose too much of the dill. Pat both fillets dry with kitchen paper and set them on a fresh sheet of clingfilm next to each other.

2 Grate the fresh beetroot and distribute this evenly over the salmon fillets. Add grated horseradish and the remainder of the dill. Drizzle a good slug of olive oil over the fillets. Place one fillet on top of the other and seal in a clingfilm parcel as for curing. Place in the refrigerator and allow to marinate for six hours. Turn the package once after three hours.

3 To serve, open the package carefully and remove the beetroot, horseradish, and dill. Slice the salmon thinly towards the tail, working from the tail end back towards the thickest part of the salmon. This style of cut is known as D slicing as the shape of the slices resembles a letter D. The top surface of the salmon will have picked up some of the colour from the beetroot and should still have lots of lovely dill flavour too.

Rinse off the excess cure.

Cover with fresh dill, beetroot, and horseradish.

Slice starting from the tail end.

TIPS

• Remember to turn the fish every 12 hours while it is curing in the salt. There is no need to unwrap it to do this.

• You don't have to use alcohol to make gravlax. This is used to give it a little extra kick, but the dish can stand up perfectly well without it.

• If you don't have clingfilm, baking parchment or greaseproof paper are great alternatives. You could also use a sealable freezer bag if you have one that is large enough.

CANAPÉ SUGGESTION

Gravlax served with a dill-infused hollandaise sauce on blinis makes a great canapé or hors d'oeuvre.

Gravlax with Honey, Mustard, and Dill Sauce

Gravlax is ideal as a starter and can be served on its own or with its traditional accompaniment – honey, mustard, and dill sauce. This sauce complements the flavour of the cured fish beautifully and is really worth a try.

INGREDIENTS

- 2 tbsp. clear honey
- 2 tbsp. wholegrain mustard
- 2 tbsp. white wine vinegar
- 5 tbsp rapeseed oil
- 2 tbsp. chopped dill
- ¼ clove of garlic (crushed)

METHOD

1 Combine the oil, vinegar, mustard, and honey in a bowl.

2 Add the crushed garlic and the chopped dill. It's as simple as that!

CURING SALMON FOR HOT-SMOKING

Most smoked foods benefit from being cured in a salt brine before they are smoked. Here the focus is on brine-curing a salmon prior to hot smoking. This is a slightly different method than that used for Scottish-style smoked salmon (page 158).

KEY STAGES

1 Brining

2 Rinsing

3 Drying

Brining Methods

The brine for this process is simply made by dissolving salt in fresh water. Additional preservatives such as Prague Powders or saltpetre are not necessary as the fish will later be cooked to a temperature high enough to destroy bacteria. Two methods of brining are described here – the choice of technique is a matter of personal preference.

Equalization brining is a technique that is used by many chefs to add flavour to their cooked meats, and works well with hot-smoked salmon. The term equalization brining refers to fact that in this method, the salt in the brine solution becomes equal to the salt concentration in the fish or meat being brined. This typically is used with very light brine solutions where the amount of salt in the food needs to be regulated closely. Using this method it is impossible for the fish to become overbrined.

Having brined your salmon using one of these methods, you are now ready to embark on hot-smoking as described on page 172.

Brining is an essential preparation for creating delicious hot-smoked salmon.

Brining – Regular Method

1 Make up a sufficient volume of strong brine in the proportion of 4 litres (8½ pints) of water to 1 kg (2¼ lb) of salt to cover your fish. Dissolve the salt in the water and chill it to 3°C (37°F) or colder before use. You can add ice as a proportion of the water to hasten cooling. The salt will cause the ice to melt as it is added to the brine. The low temperature helps reduce bacterial growth and supports the uptake of salt within the salmon.

2 Place the fish in the brine for 15 to 30 minutes, depending on the desired taste. Keep fish in the refrigerator during brining to keep the temperature as low as possible.

3 At the end of the brining time, rinse the fish thoroughly in cold water to remove excess salt from the surface.

4 Pat the fish dry with kitchen paper. It is now ready to be hot smoked.

Brining – Equalization Method

1 When using this technique, always use a similar weight of fish and water; you don't need a gallon of brine for a pound of fish. Here the instructions are to brine a 500 g (1¼ lb) piece of salmon to 2 per cent salt content, which is a light cure.

2 Place the brining container onto the scales and zero the scales. Place the salmon to be cured into the brining container. Then add water until the total combined weight of the fish and the water weighs 1 kg (2½ lb). At this point you need to calculate 2 per cent of this weight – in this case, 20 g (¾ oz).

3 Remove the salmon from the container and add the salt to the water stirring it to dissolve. Replace the salmon in the container, cover, and place in the refrigerator. Cure for 24 hours. Remove the fish from the brine and pat it dry with kitchen paper. The fish is now ready for smoking.

Make up the brine.

Allow the fish to brine for the alloted time.

TIPS

• Always keep brine in the refrigerator so its temperature is around 4°C (39°F) when used.

• Make a volume of brine that is similar to the amount of salmon you're brining. Always make enough brine for whatever you're curing. Salt is a cheap ingredient and to make a little extra is far better than not making enough.

• When using the equalization method, calculate quantities carefully to ensure tasty results.

VIRGINIA-STYLE HAM

This is a dry-cured ham in a style that
originates from Virginia, but which in turn is
based on the Westphalia hams from Germany
where delicious ham of this type has been
made for centuries.

KEY STAGES

1 Curing

2 Soaking

3 Smoking and maturing

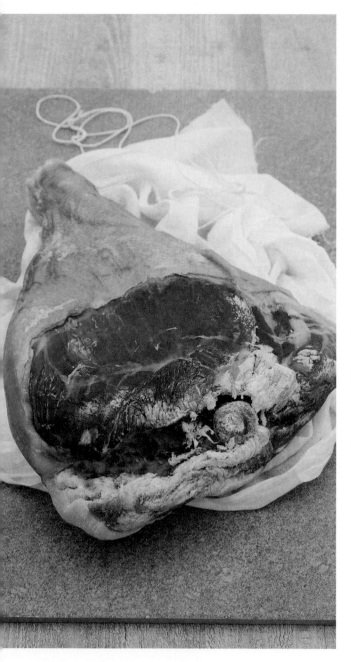

When buying the meat, go for the short-cut
ham (that's one with the gammon removed),
as this leaves less meat exposed at the hip joint
and the leg appears more square at the hip. I would
recommend a ham of around 6.5 kg (14½ lb) –
certainly no larger than 8 kg (17½ lb) in weight.

YOU WILL NEED

A whole leg of pork (trotter and aitch
bone removed).

FOR THE CURE
- 525 g (1 lb 3 oz) salt
- 125 g (4 oz) sugar
- 3 tsp. Prague Powder #2

Curing the Ham

1 Mix all the cure ingredients together and reserve half the amount. Place the ham in a nonreactive container and massage half the cure well into the ham. Use at least four fifths to cover the meat surfaces and rub the remainder into the fat and skin Make sure the shank end and the deep cavity that housed the hip joint are well covered as well.

2 Work out the cure time by allowing three days for every 1 kg (2¼ lb) in weight plus two days. So a 6.5 kg (14½ lb) ham will need to be cured for around three weeks.

3 After the first week remove the ham from the refrigerator and rub in the remainder of the cure in the same ratios as before. Return the ham to the refrigerator and continue curing for the full duration.

4 At the end of the curing period, remove the ham from the refrigerator and brush off the salt. Place the ham in a container of cool water and allow it to soak for about two hours. Dry the ham with kitchen paper and allow to rest for a day in the refrigerator.

Smoking and Maturing

1 At this stage you can choose to cold smoke the ham (see below right) or leave it unsmoked. If you choose not to smoke it, apply a mixture of herbs (see below) to all surfaces of the meat, which will give it a protective layer. Allow the ham to dry for a further two days in the refrigerator.

2 Wrap the ham in undyed muslin secured with string and hang it in a cool dry place to continue drying and maturing for up to two years. Aim to keep it at a maximum temperature of 15°C (60°F) with a relative humidity 60–70 per cent.

Apply the cure to the ham.

After a week apply the rest of the cure mix.

HERB MIX FOR UNSMOKED HAM

125 g (4 oz) cracked black pepper
450 g (1 lb) treacle
50 g (2 oz) brown sugar
3 tsp. Prague Powder #2
2 tsp. cayenne pepper

COLD SMOKING THE HAM

If you choose to cold smoke your ham, refer to pages 132–157 before you start. Hang the ham in the smoker using fruit wood or oak for up to three days. As the ham is smoked to a lovely golden colour, it will continue to dry out. Check that the temperature of the smoker remains below 30°C (80°F) for the duration of the smoking. When the smoking is complete, wrap the ham in undyed muslin and leave to mature as described for the non-smoked version.

DRY-CURED BACON

Dry-cured bacon is quite a different product than most supermarket-bought bacon, which has been injection-brined to speed up the curing process. The intensity of flavour that you get with the dry-cured version is unrivaled.

KEY STAGES

1 Curing

2 Drying

Homemade dry-cured bacon fries nicely in the pan without releasing water, unlike its mass-produced cousin, which when fried creates a large amount of water in the bottom of the pan and effectively poaches your bacon. Dry curing also has the additional benefit of enabling the bacon to last a little longer in the refrigerator.

Applying the Cure Mix

As a general rule, when applying salt to any meat to cure it, ensure that you distribute the curing mixture evenly across the surface. But if you intend to cure the bacon with the rind on, apply most of the cure mixture to the lean surface and sides of the meat and only a little to the skin side, which will only absorb a small proportion of the cure. If you aim to cure the bacon with the rind off, you can apply a little more to the fat side, which will be more receptive to the cure mixture than if it were covered by skin.

Dry-cured bacon is delicious as a breakfast dish or as a tasty addition to soups and stews.

YOU WILL NEED

- 1 kg (2¼ lb) belly pork or loin

FOR THE CURE

- 1½ tbsp. kosher salt or sea salt
- ½ tsp. Prague Powder #1

Removing the Skin

If you don't feel confident enough to remove the skin from the pork before curing, you can ask your butcher to do this for you. If you want to attempt this yourself, it is vital to use a sharp knife and ensure that the meat is extremely cold. I recommend placing the meat skin-side down on a flat board and placing it in the freezer for a short while before attempting to remove the skin This makes the fat firm, making it easier to cut between the skin and the fat.

A SWEETER CURE

If you prefer a sweeter taste to your bacon, you can add sugar, honey, or treacle to the finished bacon (see also Cold-Smoked Bacon, page 168). You can also add spices and herbs to the cure to give it extra flavour and interest.

Dry-Curing Bacon

1 Remove the rind, if you wish, from the pork and place it in a nonreactive dish.

2 Apply the cure. Use 90 per cent of the cure on the lean surface and sides of the meat if you've left the skin on, and just 10 per cent to the skin side. If you've removed the skin, apply 75 per cent of the cure to the lean surface and sides and the remaining 25 per cent to the fat side. Cover the dish with clingfilm.

3 To calculate the curing time, allow one day per 13 mm (½ inch) of thickness plus two days. Make sure you note when you started curing. While the meat is curing, store it at 2–4°C (36–40°F) in the refrigerator and turn it every day. During the curing process the pork will release some of its moisture. This will combine with the cure mix and form a strong brine solution. That is why it's important to keep turning the meat daily so the brine can work on both sides.

4 When the curing time is up, briefly rinse the meat, and pat it dry with kitchen paper. Leave the meat to dry in the refrigerator on an uncovered dish for two days. Make sure your refrigerator is free from strong flavours or smells during this time, as these may affect the flavour of the bacon. This two-day drying period allows the cure to equalize throughout the whole piece of bacon and, at the same time, it firms up the texture of the flesh.

Apply the cure mixture to the meat.

Cover the dish with clingfilm.

TYING A BUTCHER'S KNOT

When preparing a variety of cured and smoked meats such as bresaola (facing page) or pancetta (page 106), it's an advantage to be able to tie a butcher's knot, which keeps the meat securely in the shape that you want.

HOW TO TIE A BUTCHER'S KNOT

Practise this useful knot on a rolled up towel to perfect the technique.

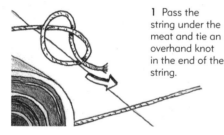

1 Pass the string under the meat and tie an overhand knot in the end of the string.

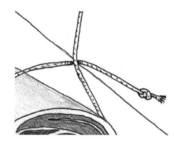

2 Pass the knotted end around the back of the other (free) end of the string and loop it back on itself.

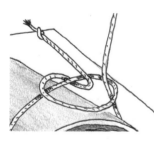

3 Using the knotted end of the string, tie an overhand knot around the free end of the string. Pull lightly to close the overhand knot but don't tighten the knot.

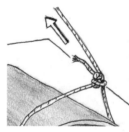

4 Pull on the free end of the string so it brings the knot in firm contact with the meat. Not too tight at first as you'll want to position the knot so it sits at the top of the meat.

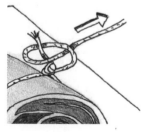

5 When you're happy the knot is in the right place, pull it tighter in jerky movements until it is secure. Lock the knot in place with a half hitch (a loop) over the knot.

6 Pull the half hitch tightly and then trim the ends with scissors.

BRESAOLA

This dark-coloured and aromatic air-dried beef is cured with salt and herbs. Made from a lean topside of beef, it's enjoyable to make and delicious to eat.

KEY STAGES

1 Preparing and curing

2 Tying

3 Drying

Bresaola originates from the northern part of Italy. The traditional cut of beef for bresaola is the topside, a muscle from the top of the back leg of the cow. Lean and dense, this whole muscle is perfect for curing and air drying.

Added Flavour

Herbs and slices are used to add flavour to the meat while it's curing in salt. You can vary the flavourings; but personally I prefer the traditional bresaola, cured with salt, sugar, juniper, pepper, rosemary, thyme, and a light grating of nutmeg.

Preparation Basics

The muscle used for bresaola is very lean but it does have some sinew on the outside that should be removed as, if left in place, it could inhibit the curing and drying process. Traditionally the cured meat is tied before it is air-dried so the meat retains a uniformly circular shape while it dries. I recommend that you use a traditional butcher's knot, which tightens as you pull and remains tight while you lock it off. But any knot will do providing it is tight enough and remains so. For instructions on tying a butcher's knot, see facing page.

Wafer-thin slices of bresaola provide a colourful and flavourful centrepiece for any charcuterie board.

Preparing and Curing the Meat

1 Start by removing any external fat, sinew, and silver skin from the surface of the meat. You are aiming to make the meat as lean as possible.

2 Finely grind all the spices and herbs together and combine with the salt, sugar, and Prague Powder #2 in a bowl. Gently rub the mixture over the entire surface of the meat, paying particular attention to the ends.

3 Place the meat in a sealable plastic bag or vacuum bag with any remaining cure and seal. Place in the refrigerator for three days per 25 mm (1 in) of thickness, plus one day. For the size of meat specified here, this is likely to be ten days.

4 Turn the meat every day to ensure the cure gets to every part. This is crucial to the success of curing.

YOU WILL NEED
- **1.6 kg (3½ lb) topside of beef**

FOR THE CURE
- **40 g (1½ oz) salt**
- **25 g (1 oz) sugar**
- **¾ tsp. Prague Powder #2**
- **1 tsp. ground black pepper**
- **2 tsp. ground nutmeg**
- **1 medium sprig of rosemary**
- **3 small sprigs of thyme**
- **10 juniper berries (crushed)**

Rub the cure over the surface of the meat.

Seal the meat in a plastic or vacuum bag.

Tying the Meat

1 At the end of the curing time, remove the meat from the bag and pat it dry with kitchen paper.

2 Using butcher's string, tie a loop of string around the meat to hold it in shape. Secure the loop with a butcher's knot (see page 68).

3 Tie further loops at 3-cm (1½-in) intervals around the circumference of the meat along its length. Securing the final loop with another butcher's knot, and then trim the ends with scissors.

Drying

1 With the meat tied up, you have a couple of options: you can either seal the meat in a dry-aging bag or wrap it loosely in undyed muslin, securing it at the top and bottom with butcher's string, and then hang it to air dry for about a month. Before air-drying, weigh the cloth-covered meat, record this weight, and occasionally throughout the drying process, check the weight loss.

2 Keep the meat at a temperature of around 15°C (60°F) and at a relative humidity (RH) of 65–70 per cent. The meat is ready when it has lost 20–25 per cent of its original weight.

Tie the meat securely along its length.

The tied meat is ready for drying.

Wrap the meat loosely in undyed muslin.

MOULD CHECK

Don't worry about any specks of white mould on the surface of the meat. This is normal. If you see any furry, green, orange, or black mould on the surface, remove it by wiping clean with a small piece of cloth soaked in white wine vinegar.

Simply Bresaola

Bresaola is typically eaten with salads or as part of a cold cuts selection
— a tasty but light focus for a light summer lunch.

This fragrant cured beef adorns a plate with a wide variety of foods. Wherever ham can be used, so bresaola can be substituted. A classic combination is with some green leaves, balsamic vinegar, and olive oil, served with crusty bread. You could also add some thinly sliced cherry tomatoes and wafer-thin shavings of Parmesan cheese. Make sure you slice the bresaola as thinly as possible so it literally melts in the mouth.

DRY-CURED VENISON

A game meat with a distinctive flavour, venison is often considered the prince of meats. It is wonderfully lean, which makes it a great candidate for transformation into an Italian-style air-dried delicacy.

KEY STAGES

1 Preparation

2 Curing

3 Smoking

4 Drying

Air drying intensifies the already-rich flavour of venison. It also firms the texture to produce a dense and easily sliced cured meat similar to bresaola (see page 69). Curing venison in this way uses many of the same techniques used when making bresaola, but the ingredients differ and the shape of the finished product is flatter, so when it is cut across the grain, it has the finished look of prosciutto without the fat "cap". The method described here gives the venison a light cold smoking using sweet chestnut wood. The technique is similar to that used for bacon (page 168). Be sure to read the general instructions on smoking on pages 132–157 before you start. I recommend that you hang the meat from a stainless steel hook, if possible, but you'll achieve good results using a food rack.

Cure Flavours

The choice of herbs and spices to flavour venison is quite important. Juniper, rosemary, garlic, pepper, and thyme go particularly well as do some of the more exotic spices such as cloves, cinnamon, and allspice.

In my opinion, the more exotic spices have a tendency to overpower the venison if overused, but in small quantities can emphasize the natural flavour of the meat, adding just a hint of spice. The cure described here consists of typically Italian flavours, which work well with venison.

YOU WILL NEED

- **1.5 kg (3¼ lb) leg of venison**

FOR THE CURE
- **40 g (1½ oz) salt**
- **25 g (1 oz) sugar**
- **¾ tsp. Prague Powder #2**
- **2 cloves of garlic (crushed)**
- **1 tsp. ground black pepper**
- **1 medium sprig of fresh rosemary**
- **2 small sprigs of thyme**
- **5 bay leaves**
- **10 juniper berries (crushed)**

Choosing the Venison

The instructions here are for a 1.5 kg (3¼ lb) piece of venison from the leg. This is part of a whole muscle from the back of the leg. If you are considering air drying a whole hind leg from a smaller deer you'd be advised to follow the technique described on page 102 for air drying a ham. The herbs suggested in this cure recipe can be used with the whole hind leg techniques.

Preparation and Curing

1 Trim any sinew or silver skin from the venison so that it looks completely lean.

2 Grind all the herbs and garlic to a fine paste in a spice grinder or using a pestle and mortar. Transfer into a bowl along with the salt, sugar, and the Prague Powder #2. Mix all these ingredients together and set aside.

3 Apply the cure evenly to all sides of meat and place in a sealable bag. Allow the venison to cure in the refrigerator for seven days. Turn the meat daily to ensure the meat cures evenly.

> ### TIPS
>
> • This technique is suitable for air drying using dry-aging bags (see page 84).
>
> • If you don't have a sealable bag to cure the venison, you can securely enclose the meat in clingfilm and place the package in a glass dish in the refrigerator for the specified time. The dish will catch any unwanted leaks.

4 When the curing time is over, remove the venison from the refrigerator and rinse lightly under cold, running water. Pat the meat dry with kitchen paper, weigh it, and record the weight.

5 Return the cured venison (uncovered) to the refrigerator for 24 hours to dry. While it is drying, a sticky surface (pellicle) will form, which will help the smoke to stick.

Trim sinew and silver skin from the meat.

Prepare the cure ingredients.

Smoking and Drying

1 Cold smoke the venison for 8–12 hours. This will achieve a delicate coating of smoke, which will help to protect the meat while it air dries.

2 When the venison has been smoked, remove it from the smoker. Loosely wrap it in undyed muslin and secure it with butcher's string. Hang it up to air dry for three months or until it has lost 20–25 per cent of its pre-drying weight. The conditions for air drying should be 65–75 per cent relative humidity and a temperature of around 15°C (60°F). Alternatively, use dry-aging bags for this part of the process (see page 84). Read pages 76–87 for more information on drying techniques.

3 Check the meat at regular intervals while it is curing. If it smells wrong, then it probably is wrong and may need closer inspection. Expect to see a white bloom on the surface of the meat. Remove any black, green, orange or furry material from the surface with a clean cloth and wipe the problem area with white wine vinegar. This will promote the growth of helpful bacteria. When the meat has reached its target weight, remove the muslin and inspect the surface. Cut away any obviously dry pieces and slice across the grain to reveal a deep reddish purple meat with a lovely dense texture and aromatic flavour. To store, either vacuum pack in the refrigerator for up to a month or freeze for up to three months. Serve very thinly sliced.

Apply the cure to the surface of the meat.

Dry-aging bags can be used to dry the venison.

Serving Dry-Cured Venison

Dry-cured venison has a delicate flavour even though its appearance and colour might suggest otherwise.

Served on a bed of green leaves with shavings of Parmesan cheese, it needs no more complicated preparation. However, you can lend this simple venison salad an extra dimension by serving it with a vinaigrette dressing or some red onion chutney. You can give your vinaigrette an extra kick by infusing the oil with a spoon of cracked black pepper and lemon peel for up to a month. To get the full effect, it's a good idea to start to infuse your oil at the same time as you begin to air dry the venison.

Drying Meat and Fish

DRYING: AN INTRODUCTION

Drying as a means of preserving food is a technique that has been practised for millennia and is still widely used today. As well as keeping food from spoiling, where the climate is warm, the sun's energy can also be used to make the flavours more intense.

Bacteria and mould cannot flourish in dry conditions, and this is the principal reason why drying works as a food preservation technique. However, achieving the right degree of dryness is a balancing act that usually requires a little practice to get just right; too dry and the food may be inedible and too wet and the food is likely to spoil.

Vegetables and fruit can simply be dried in the sun and require no other ingredients to preserve them. This is not always the case with meat and fish. Most meat and fish need to be salted before they are left to dry. To leave raw meat and fish out in the sun to dry without the application of salt could provide the right conditions for dangerous bacteria to multiply, creating a health risk for consumers. For more information on the use of salt, see pages 18–20.

Air-drying requires certain conditions to work properly. Ideally the relative humidity (RH) should be between 65 and 75 per cent and the temperature should be between 12°C and 18°C (54–65°F). Under these conditions, you will give yourself the best chance of success when you dry meat and fish.

Warmth and Breezes

Techniques for drying food seem to be more widely used in hotter climates where the sun's energy is able to dry food more directly than in some of the more temperate regions of the globe. The famous prosciutto di Parma (Parma ham) is an exception to this rule. This delicacy is produced in northern Italy where cool, dry breezes descending from the mountains do the main work of drying this delicious ham (see also Air-Dried Ham, page 102). The movement of air is a key part of the food-drying process as it promotes moisture loss through surface evaporation.

Extreme Drying

Drying includes another process known as "desiccation", which removes virtually all the moisture. One well-known food that is desiccated is salt cod, which is described on page 126. This cod product is dried until it is very dense and is inedible without rehydration. This also means it can be stored for long periods of time without spoiling.

Modern Approaches

Modern tools and equipment have made a simple process even easier. Traditional methods for making jerky, for example, used to involve the use of wooden frames on which the meat was hung to dry in the sun. Nowadays purpose-made food dehydrators are readily available for home use. Commercial operations and some forward-thinking home producers have started using dry-aging bags, which allow drying to take place in a temperature-controlled environment such as a cold room or refrigerator. This is a huge leap forwards for the home practitioner and food industry alike as it avoids the need for expensive conditioning rooms and large energy bills, and enables you to manage the humidity and temperature easily. These bags also protect the food from airborne bacteria (see also page 84).

Coppa cured in the Italian style is an impressive and flavoursome charcuterie treat.

HOW DRYING WORKS

Drying food can make it last a lot longer than brining or dry salting alone, and it has other benefits too. To make the most of this technique, you need to understand how it works.

Meat and fish can be preserved effectively by air drying, but these foods must first be treated with salt. Dry salting using rubs or by packing the meat or fish in salt removes much of the moisture within the flesh rapidly, which gives the overall drying and preservation process a head start. Equally importantly, salt discourages bacterial growth, giving an extra protection against spoilage.

The Role of Marinating

There are a few air-dried products that don't involve dry salting, rather they are treated with flavourings (marinated) before being dried. One good example of this is jerky. Jerky is made from thin strips of meat, which if dry-salted prior to drying, would become almost inedible. The marinade for jerky provides seasonings and flavourings with a little salt in it. The primary mechanisms for maintaining a

safe, finished jerky product are rapid drying and, of course, fresh meat to work with in the first place.

Understanding the Variables

Although the removal of moisture may sound like a reasonably simple process, there are a number of things to think about. Much depends on the size, thickness, texture, and density of the meat to be treated. This makes drying a little more complex than it may at first seem. Large pieces of meat will take time to dry because moisture in the centre of the meat or fish takes longer to diffuse to the edges where it can be lost to the surrounding atmosphere.

Weight Loss and Humidity

In order to dry meat and fish to the point where it can be eaten safely without the need to cook it, you need to assess the moisture loss as a percentage of

Marinating is usually recommended before drying.

Dry-aging bags are a convenient aid to producing dried foods.

Thin strips of duck will dry relatively quickly.

the fresh weight. One of the easiest ways to judge when your meat or fish have dried sufficiently is to compare the starting weight with the finished weight. A weight loss of 20–30 per cent is generally enough to render meat and fish safe to eat raw. Jerky and biltong are examples of products that are dried beyond this level, but some air-dried meats such as air-dried ham and air-dried duck require only 20–25 per cent weight loss.

The relative humidity (RH) plays a large part in the drying process. Case hardening (see right), is likely to occur if the meat is dried in an environment that is too dry or has a low RH. Conversely, the meat or fish is unlikely to dry sufficiently in an environment that is too damp or has a very high RH. This may sound obvious but in some parts of the world the weather conditions can make drying naturally virtually impossible because of the high humidity. In these conditions the only way to dry food is by using a conditioning room, food dehydrator, or dry-aging bags.

ABOUT CASE HARDENING

Attempting to hasten the drying process can lead to case hardening, in which a nearly impermeable shell forms on the outside of the meat or fish. This effectively retards the drying process by preventing moisture in the centre getting out through the hard outer layer. To reverse case hardening, the meat or fish can be placed in a sealed environment, where the moisture inside the food can eventually rehydrate the hardened outer surface from within. This process can take some time and it's always better to air dry under the most favourable conditions to avoid the problem in the first place. Bear in mind that thicker cuts of meat such as those used for biltong are the most prone to case hardening.

EQUIPMENT YOU WILL NEED

If you are new to this process, it's likely that you are going to need some equipment to dry food. Personally, I like to try to make use of existing equipment, but sometimes it's worth making the investment to get the right kit for the job.

Drying food can be as simple as hanging something out to dry or as complicated as measuring humidity and temperature and recording data in drying graphs. The latter is outside the scope of this book, and the methods recommended won't involve expensive equipment. If you have access to a fan oven, for example, you can achieve excellent results at a fraction of the cost of a commercial dehydrator. The items described on these pages are those most useful for drying food at home.

Thermometer

A good digital thermometer can be obtained from any good cookware shop or online at a modest cost. This is an essential piece of kit in assessing the correct conditions for air drying.

RH Meter

Relative humidity (RH) is one of the measurements that you need to monitor. A meter can be bought online. Some models have a built-in thermometer, which may be convenient. You can use this device to check the conditions in your conditioning room and even in your refrigerator.

Weighing Scales

These are essential for checking the weight before and after salting and drying and are useful for weighing ingredients. Digital scales that can accommodate a large bowl and models that can weigh up to 5 kg (11 lb) are the most useful. If you intend to weigh very small quantities (for example, of curing salts that require a degree of accuracy), I recommend precision scales that measure to either

to two decimal places or fractions of an ounce. These are available from good cookware shops or online. For measuring small quantities of dry or liquid ingredients, a set of accurate measuring spoons is invaluable.

Dry-Aging Bags

These bags are a relatively new concept and are gaining in popularity. You will also need a food saver-type vacuum machine (see below). These allow you to air dry in the refrigerator, removing the need for a conditioning room. For more information, see page 84.

Food-Saver Vacuum Machine

This is one of the best purchases I have made in recent years. This item can assist in the storage of dried products such as jerky and biltong in vacuum bags, saving on waste due to spoilage. It can also be used with dry-aging bags.

Food-Saver Bags

These bags come in a roll or in packs of various sizes and are specifically designed for use with the food-saver vacuum machine.

Meat Hooks

Useful for suspending meat, especially when you regularly need to take down items for weighing. Handling heavier cuts is easier if you use hooks rather than relying on tying them up with string.

String, Netting, and Racks

Butcher's string or twine is very strong and also food grade. It has multiple uses for securing meat

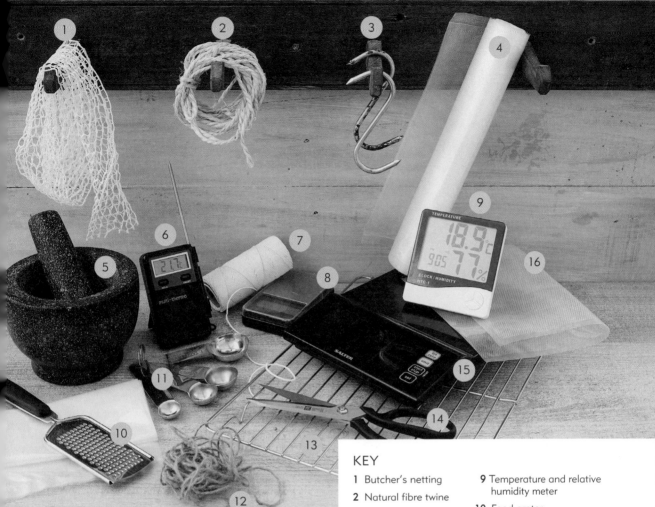

KEY

1 Butcher's netting
2 Natural fibre twine
3 Meat hooks
4 Food saver bags
5 Pestle and mortar
6 Meat thermometer
7 Butcher's string
8 Precision scales

9 Temperature and relative humidity meter
10 Food grater
11 Measuring spoons
12 Twine
13 Food rack
14 Scissors
15 Digital scales
16 Dry-aging bag

during drying. Other types of twine are useful for hanging meat during drying. Butcher's netting is useful for securing some types of dried meat during the drying process. Other products are dried flat on wire food racks.

Scissors

A good pair of scissors is a must. Useful for cutting string and trimming vacuum bags on a roll. Don't skimp on a cheap pair; you get what you pay for.

Grinders and Graters

Many of the ingredients for dry rubs, marinades, and brines need to be grated or ground to release their flavours. You'll need a good grater and a pestle and mortar to prepare these.

CONDITIONING ROOM

This is a place where you have control over temperature and humidity. You need a room fitted with a means to cool or heat the room, and some form of humidity control. This is not a cheap option. If you have a cool, moist cellar in the house or a suitable outbuilding that will allow you to maintain the drying parameters, then you're in luck.

DRY-AGING BAGS

Dry-aging bags have revolutionized the practice of preserving meat and fish by making this once artisan craft more accessible than ever before. In the past specialist charcutiers had to create conditioning rooms with expensively controlled environments to keep their products safe during drying. Using these bags, you can now air dry meat and fish safely in a domestic refrigerator.

The use of dry-aging bags is relatively new. But there are increasing numbers of users who see the benefits of drying meat in a bag without the expense of a purpose-built room. These bags remove the need to worry about levels of heat and humidity as you can air dry in the refrigerator.

How They Work

Dry-aging bags are made from a specially designed plastic film that is permeable by both moisture and oxygen. This plastic membrane is food grade and works in a similar way to the breathable fabrics used in sportswear. These bags are a little more expensive than traditional high-quality vacuum bags and need to be used in conjunction with a food-saver vacuum machine. The food-filled bags have to be in a reasonably dry environment, such as that provided by a domestic refrigerator, to work effectively. In addition to drying, you can also smoke meat and fish in dry-aging bags. The compounds in the smoke are able to permeate the membrane imparting their flavour to the food.

Dry-aging bags come in various sizes. Larger sizes can be used to dry age a boneless joint of beef or lamb. The smaller sizes are ideal for smaller cuts of meat such steaks, pork loin, rolled pancetta, or duck breasts.

Using Dry-Aging Bags

After filling a dry-aging bag, you'll need to remove as much air from the bag as possible before sealing it. To facilitate air removal with a vacuum machine, these bags come with a "vac-assist strip", which is inserted into the top of the bag. Insert the vac assist into the mouth of the bag leaving a little of the vac-assist strip protruding from the bag. This is important as the bag will have a tendency to flatten when the vacuum is pulled. The point of the vac-assist strip is to maintain a small air gap so the vacuum machine can still work to expel the air from the bag. It is important that the vac-assist strip crosses the heat sealing bar as this is another point where the machine can have difficulty in removing the air from the bag.

Don't worry too much if you seem to achieve a good vacuum one day and the day after it looks as if the vacuum has been lost a little. This is normal because the bags aren't true vacuum bags. The vacuum serves to make a sound contact between the bag and the meat to aid drying. The bag needs to be in contact with the meat for only about a day before it forms a bond and will remain in contact for the duration of the drying.

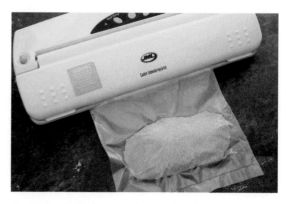

Dry-aging bags need to be used with a vacuum machine.

ADDING FLAVOUR

Some types of dried meat require the addition of flavour – from delicate and subtle notes to robust and hot spiciness – before drying. This chapter looks at how this can be achieved and at what stage the different flavours should be added.

Flavourings are often incorporated into salted meats and fish before they are dried, usually at the same time as salting, when herbs, spices, and sweetening agents are incorporated into the salt mixture. A great example of this is jerky (see page 88) where the meat is liberally coated in a wide variety of flavourings before drying. It may seem obvious, but when meat and fish become dry, they are less able to absorb flavours, so to do this before drying makes complete sense.

Rubs and Marinades

Flavours can be added dry as a dry rub, a blend of salt, sweeteners, spices, and herbs or as a wet marinade, often consisting of juices, sauces, alcohol, honey, and oils. These all add flavour or can act as a carrier for flavours. Dry rubs are useful for adding flavour before drying because they are also mixed with a small amount of salt, which draws moisture from the meat and in turn rehydrates the dry rub allowing it to soak into the meat. These dry rubs are easy to create and are widely used to add flavour to barbecued and hot-smoked food.

About Herbs and Spices

The addition of herbs and spices is an age-old way of giving new flavours to meat and fish. Leafy herbs such as sage and thyme work really well in marinades and rubs. Herbs and spices in the form of seeds need a little encouragement before releasing their flavours. If you really want to get the best from seeds, try lightly roasting them in a small frying pan. Mustard, peppercorns, lavender, fennel, and caraway are examples of seeds that work really well when lightly roasted. After roasting, crush the

> ### TIPS
>
> • Add flavourings, spices, and sweeteners to the curing mix or marinade before drying.
>
> • Lightly roast herbs and spice seeds before adding them to your rub, marinade, or cure.
>
> • Dried herbs can be more pungent than the same weight of their fresh equivalent. Gauge the amount you use carefully.

casings of the seeds to allow all the aromatic oils to infuse into the rub or marinade. You'll find that using this method will impart a lot more flavour into your foods. An added bonus when you treat seeds in this way is that you need smaller quantities.

How Much Do You Need?

There are no hard and fast rules to follow for the quantity of herbs or spices to add for a given quantity of meat or fish. However, it's worth bearing in mind that some dried herbs tend to have a lot more punch for their weight when compared to their fresh equivalent. This is particularly true of dried thyme, basil, and sage. Some of the oriental spices such as cloves, cinnamon, and star anise have a strong flavour and should be used sparingly. Typically, I would use only about half a teaspoon of cloves and cinnamon to make a dry rub for a 1 kg (2¼ lb) piece of pork belly for use in making bacon.

DRYING TIMES

When drying food, it's vital to know when the drying process is complete in order to be absolutely sure that the food is safe to eat. Observing tried and tested guidelines on both drying time and weight (moisture loss) will ensure that your food is properly prepared.

The easiest way to gauge how drying is progressing is to measure the weight loss as a percentage of the starting weight. The other measure of moisture in food used by food scientists is known as water activity; in simple terms this is a measure of vapour pressure in a product divided by the standard water vapour pressure. There are plenty of detailed explanations of this measure online, but its enough to mention that water activity is correlated to bacterial growth in foods and not necessarily the moisture content specifically. Measuring water activity is difficult for the home producer as it requires special resistance measuring equipment. For this reason using percentage weight loss is a more accurate and practical method of determining when your meat or fish is dried sufficiently.

DRYING GUIDELINES

These times and weight loss estimates are approximate.
Follow the detailed guidance for specific products later in this chapter.

AIR-DRIED PRODUCT	TIME TO DRY	WEIGHT LOSS
Biltong	7–10 days	65–75%
Salt cod	7–14 days	30–40%
Chorizo	21–28 days	17–23%
Coppa	2–3 months	20–25%
Duck	5–7 days	10–15%
Jerky	1 day	50–60%
Lamb	3–6 months	20–25%
Mackerel	5–7 days	25–35%
Prosciutto	6–24 months	15–25%
Salami	1–3 months	20–25%
Venison	2–3 months	25–30%

SLICING AND STORING

When you've spent time and effort transforming meat and fish by drying and/or smoking, you'll want to be able to slice your product so it looks at its best. And you'll want to store it in a way that preserves both the look and flavours you've worked so hard to achieve.

Some of the foods you'll produce will already be sliced thinly – jerky, for instance – others such as air-dried ham or dry-cured venison are likely to need slicing before you can serve them and in many cases before you can store them too.

Slicing Equipment

There are some really good domestic meat slicers on the market, which won't be nearly as expensive as a commercial meat slicer. For most home meat preserving operations, a basic slicer is all you need, and is capable of slicing chorizo, salami, and possibly some smaller hams and gammons.

If you choose to hand slice air-dried hams, coppa, bresaola, air-dried duck, and similar meats, it may be worth investing in a good-quality slicing knife instead. I find a fluted carving knife works well as the product is less likely to stick to the blade as you cut. Also, because the knife has a thin blade, it is easy to control – a distinct advantage when aiming for wafer-thin slices.

Freezing Essentials

When it comes to storing your product, in my opinion, you can't do better than to vacuum pack and freeze. Given the time and effort that you will have put into producing it, you owe it to the product to treat it in a way that preserves its quality. With air-dried hams, for instance, you'll be preserving the meat's moisture content when it's sliced and vacuum-packed so it will remain in prime condition. Most dried meat products freeze well. This is due mainly to their low moisture content. These products can last for up to a year in a good freezer (one that maintains a temperature of -20°C /-4°F).

A selection of sharp knives is an asset.

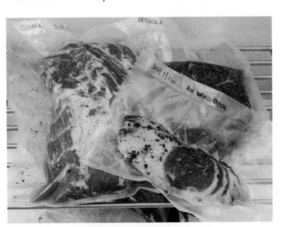

Freezing is an excellent method for storing dried meat and fish.

LABELLING

When you freeze food, always label it with a description of what it is and the date you bagged it. If you don't have any labels or you are worried labels will fall off, buy a permanent marker pen that can write onto plastic.

BEEF JERKY

In warm climates drying is the traditional way of preserving meat. One of the best-known examples of this preservation method is the popular and tasty snack, jerky. Any lean meat can be preserved in this way, but perhaps the best-known is beef jerky.

Beef jerky is typically made from topside of beef and is sliced into thin strips before being dried. Jerky is usually marinated in various flavourings before drying to add a little kick to it. Worcestershire sauce, soy sauce, pepper, paprika, onion, and a little salt and sugar are examples of the flavourings that can be added to the marinade.

Keep It Lean

The leaner the meat the better; fatty meats have a tendency to become rancid over a short period of time especially when exposed to warmer temperatures. It is important when making jerky to remove any visible fat from the meat before drying. This is why jerky made from cuts of venison and quality cuts of lean beef are so popular.

Drying the Meat

In the past jerky was dried by leaving meat to hang over a wooden frame to dry in the warmth of the sunshine. Nowadays drying is usually carried out in an oven or dehydrator. Drying jerky is a reasonably simple process. It can be achieved in an oven set at a low temperature – around 50°C (120°F) – with the door left slightly open.

Tasty strips of beef jerky can provide a flavoursome and sustaining snack.

Preparing and Marinating the Meat

1 Use a sharp knife to remove visible sinew and fat from the meat. Cut the meat into thin strips. To make the finished jerky easier to chew, cut across the grain of the muscle. It is easier to slice the meat when it has been partially frozen as it tends to hold its shape better. Partially frozen meat can usually be passed through a meat slicer to get really thin and even slices. But you may prefer (as I do) to cut the strips by hand as this saves on cleaning a machine.

2 Mix all the ingredients of your chosen marinade recipe together in a bowl and add the strips of beef. Mix well to coat them completely. Cover with clingfilm and allow the meat to marinate in the refrigerator for 24 hours.

Trim fat and visible sinew from the surface of the meat.

YOU WILL NEED
- **1 kg (2 lb) topside of beef**

FOR THE MARINADE
- **1 tsp. black peppercorns (crushed)**
- **1 tsp. garlic powder**
- **1 tsp. cayenne pepper**
- **1 tsp. chilli powder**
- **2 tsp. onion powder or half a small onion (grated)**
- **5 tsp. light soy sauce**
- **3 tbsp. Worcestershire sauce**
- **1 tsp. sugar or honey (optional)**

Jerky Essentials

You can substitute any other lean meat for the beef specified here. Sugar is used extensively in the modern-day commercially produced jerky, and personally, I think the addition of a little sweetness can be a good thing but ultimately it comes down to personal taste.

Slice the meat very thinly.

Drying

1 Remove the meat from the marinade and arrange the strips of beef on a wire rack, keeping them separate from each other and as flat as possible.

2 Set the oven at 50°C (120°F) and place the loaded wire racks in the oven. Keep the door of the oven slightly open to allow the moisture in the meat to evaporate. This should take about 4 to 5 hours to complete. The drying time will be quicker if you use a fan oven.

3 Check the meat every half hour and rearrange the racks so the meat dries evenly. You'll notice as the meat dries, it darkens in colour and shrinks a little. Your jerky is done when it is dry to the point where the meat shows some resistance to bending but does not snap. If the meat snaps, this indicates that it has become over dry.

Remove the meat from the marinade.

Dry the strips on a wire rack in the oven.

Check the jerky is dry but still pliable.

ALTERNATIVE FLAVOURS

The following alternative jerky marinades will flavour 1 kg (2 lb) topside of beef, using the method described in this section.

TERIYAKI-STYLE JERKY
1 tsp. black peppercorns (crushed)
1 tsp. garlic powder
1 tsp. cayenne pepper
Half a small onion (grated)
3 tbsp. teriyaki sauce
5 tsp. Worcestershire sauce
2 tsp. sugar or honey (optional)

SWEET AND SOUR JERKY
100 ml (½ cup) white wine vinegar
2 tbsp. lemon juice
1 tbsp. soy sauce
1 tbsp. tomato ketchup
½ tbsp. honey
1 tsp. garlic powder
1 tsp. black peppercorns (crushed)
1 tsp. chilli powder
1 tsp. smoked paprika

DUCK JERKY

Duck jerky is an excellent alternative to beef jerky and is a little more tender to chew. The variations for this form of jerky are numerous and you'll find some ideas here.

Duck is a versatile and widely available meat that has many uses. One of my favourite ways of preparing duck is to turn it into duck jerky. It's slightly milder than beef and takes on added flavourings really well. And it's a lot easier to remove the fat from duck than from many other meats.

The jerky method is a delicious way to create a tasty snack from duck breasts.

YOU WILL NEED
- 1 kg (2¼ lb) skinless duck breast

FOR THE BASIC MARINADE
- 1 tbsp. salt
- 1½ tbsp. sugar
- 150 ml (5 fl. oz) light soy sauce

BE SAFE

Be sure to avoid the possibility of E-coli poisoning by drying the duck or goose meat in the oven after marinating in the same way as for beef jerky (page 90)

Cut the meat into strips.

Making Duck Jerky

1 De-skin the duck and remove any connective tissue and silver skin leaving a lean breast. Slice the duck breast into thin strips.

2 Spread them out on a firm wooden board and cover them in a layer of clingfilm. Flatten the slices with a rolling pin or the base of a small saucepan. When you've done this you're ready to marinate the duck.

3 Make up the marinade of your choice (a variety of options are given on the facing page), and continue as described for beef jerky (page 89).

Flatten the strips with a rolling pin

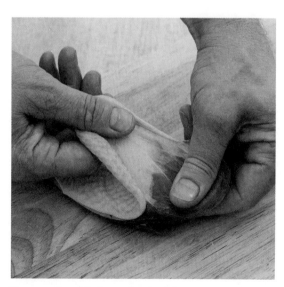

Remove the skin from the duck breast.

Put the meat in the marinade.

ALTERNATIVE FLAVOURS

Add these alternative flavour combinations to the basic marinade. If you choose to add any liquid ingredients, subtract the same amount of light soy sauce. Remember that the specified amounts are for marinating 1 kg (2¼ lb) of duck. If you're making a larger batch, you'll need to increase the amount of marinade proportionately.

SPICY TERIYAKI DUCK JERKY (1)
5 tsp. teriyaki sauce
1 tsp. chilli powder
1 tsp. ground black pepper

SEASONAL DUCK JERKY (2)
1 tsp. ground star anise
1 tsp. ground cinnamon
5 tsp. Scotch whisky

CHINESE-STYLE DUCK JERKY (3)
1 tsp. Chinese five spice
5 tsp. white wine vinegar

SPICY CHILLI DUCK JERKY (4)
5 tsp. Worcestershire sauce
1 tsp. chilli powder
½ tsp. cayenne pepper
1 tsp. garlic powder
½ tsp. ground black pepper

FRUITY DUCK JERKY (5)
1 tsp. crushed juniper berries
Zest and juice of half an orange
½ tsp. dried thyme

GOOSE JERKY

The rich meat of a goose makes excellent jerky and works well with many of the flavour combinations as suggested for duck jerky. Certain breeds of goose have fat marbling in their breast meat and should be avoided when making jerky if you are planning to keep the meat for any length of time. If you choose to consume it quickly or vacuum pack it and freeze it, then you can use any type of goose. Ask your supplier for advice.

The basic marinade and technique is the same for goose jerky as it is for duck (see page 91).

BILTONG

Biltong is a traditional dried meat snack that originated in South Africa. It is similar to jerky in some respects, but the classic version is not sweetened. This will be a hugely popular snack for hikers and sports fans that is easy to make at home.

KEY STAGES

1 Preparation and curing

2 Drying and storing

Adopted by European settlers in South Africa from the indigenous peoples, biltong was traditionally made from beef but can be made from springbok, ostrich, and many other red meats and poultry. Originally, biltong would have been prepared and allowed to dry under the sun. Because biltong is made from much thicker cuts of meat than jerky (typically 50 mm/2 in) the meat can take longer to dry out completely. This works when the sun and the breeze are present in the right measures, but when this is not the case, you need to think of ways to get around this challenge.

Biltong Boxes

The biltong box is a container in which the meat can hang while a small fan (in some cases) and holes at the top and bottom of the box allow the air to circulate. The holes are usually protected against insects with a fine mesh. To raise the temperature in the box to promote drying, some biltong boxes have small, low-wattage lights in the base.

You can get the same results if you hang biltong in a refrigerator or use dry-aging bags (see page 84). It's even possible to dry biltong in the oven. This starts off the drying process and partially case hardens the meat. You can then hang the meat outside to dry naturally and it is usually ready in about three days.

Biltong can be hung to dry in the open air if the conditions are right.

Traditional biltong is cured in salt and white wine vinegar and coated with crushed coriander seeds and pepper. You can add a little chilli to give it a kick, if you like. Because biltong is classed as a slow-dried product, for safety I recommend the use of Prague Powder #2.

Preparation and Curing

1 Remove visible connective tissue, fat, and silver skin from the meat. Cut into 75-mm long (3-in) strips.

2 Pour the vinegar, salt, and Prague Powder into a bowl. Mix and add the strips of meat. Leave to marinate in the refrigerator for about two hours.

3 Crush the coriander seeds in a pestle and mortar and mix with the pepper and chilli (if using). Remove the meat from the marinade and liberally coat in the coriander mix.

Drying and Storing

Hang the strips of meat in a biltong box or lay them on racks in the oven set at the lowest possible temperature. A fan oven is best as this circulates the heat and assists the drying process. The biltong is sufficiently dry when it has gone a little dark and stiff. Store biltong in a vacuum pack for up to a year in the freezer but in my experience it is far too delicious to keep for that long.

YOU WILL NEED
- **1 kg (2¼ lb) lean topside of beef**

FOR THE MARINADE
- **100 ml (½ cup) white wine or cider vinegar**
- **1 tbsp. salt**
- **½ tsp. Prague Powder #2**

FOR THE SEASONING
- **8 tbsp. coriander seeds**
- **1 tsp. ground black pepper**
- **¼ tsp. finely chopped chilli (optional)**

Cut the meat into strips and marinate.

Coat with the dry seasoning mix.

AIR-DRIED AND SMOKED DUCK

It's true that the simplest things in life are sometimes the best, and air-dried and oak-smoked duck breasts are a great example of delicious food that is easy to make. I regularly prepare these wonderful duck breasts very lightly cold smoked over oak – the result can be quite sublime.

Air-dried duck, or duck ham as it is sometimes known, is a really interesting way of enjoying a relatively inexpensive cut of meat and is an especially good choice if you are inexperienced at air drying. The method I employ works through all the stages that you are likely to encounter when air-drying meat and is a fantastic introductory project for someone who wants to pursue air drying as a culinary hobby or just as an experiment.

Serving

Sliced thinly, duck breast prepared in this way is perfect on its own with bread or served with some cherry tomatoes or tossed in a green salad with croutons and a good French dressing. Air drying and smoking transforms a simple duck breast into a rare delicacy. I can't imagine not having this delight at my fingertips.

Air-dried and smoked duck breast is usually served thinly sliced with salad leaves.

Curing

1 Grind two tablespoons of the salt, the juniper berries, and the thyme leaves (removed from the stems) using a pestle and mortar or spice grinder. Place a tablespoon of orange zest and the remaining salt in a bowl and add the juniper, salt, and thyme. Mix well.

2 Sprinkle about a quarter of the cure mixture into the base of a nonreactive container. Place the first duck breast skin side down onto the cure and add about two thirds of the remaining cure onto the flesh side of the duck and place the second filled skin side up directly on top of the first duck breast. Add the remaining cure to the skin side of the uppermost duck breast. Cover the container with clingfilm and refrigerate.

3 After about 18 hours, remove the duck from the refrigerator and rinse each duck breast under cold running water to remove the salt. Pat dry with kitchen paper. You will notice that after curing the duck breasts will appear quite firm having lost a lot of their original moisture. Their colour will have darkened a little too.

YOU WILL NEED

- **2 duck breasts (skin on) each weighing approximately 350 g (12 oz)**

FOR THE CURE

- **50 g (2 oz) sea salt**
- **3 sprigs of thyme**
- **5 juniper berries**
- **1 tbsp. orange zest**

Sprinkle the cure mix onto the first duck breast.

Cover the skin of the second duck breast with cure mix.

Drying

1 The duck breasts are now ready to be air dried. You can choose between two methods for air drying: traditional (see below) and using dry-aging bags. The use of dry-aging bags is described on page 84. Using this method, you can dry the duck breasts in the refrigerator. It will take about two weeks, depending on the thickness of the meat, to achieve the desired reduction in weight of 15–20 per cent.

2 Whichever method you use, at the end of the drying process, the duck breasts will have firmed up, the fat will have also lost moisture and yellowed a little on the surface, and there will be a distinctive smell of charcuterie.

Cold Smoking

To finish the duck breasts, they should be placed in a smoker. Read the instructions on pages 132–157 before undertaking this. Allow the duck breasts to cold smoke over oak dust for 4 hours. This timing may seem a little short, but it's worth remembering that oak has a very strong flavour and is a heavy smoke which doesn't require a long time to create its effect. It can be true to say that less is more, especially when dealing with a delicate flavour like duck. The temperature in the smoker should not exceed 30°C (86°F). The duck breast will have retained a thin film of natural oil on its surface, which will assist in ensuring the smoke sticks to its surface. By the end of the smoking process, the skin of the duck will have darkened slightly to a light tan.

Seal the duck breast in a dry-aging bag or wrap in undyed muslin.

Remove excess air from the bag with a vacuum machine.

TRADITIONAL DRYING

The traditional method for air drying duck breasts is to loosely wrap them in squares of undyed muslin, tying the tops and bottoms with string. These are then suspended in a cool suitably moist atmosphere to dry for one to two weeks. The muslin provides protection from flies and other pests.

Air-Dried and Smoked Duck Salad

This style of duck breast can be eaten alone as a starter or can be served as part of a charcuterie platter with a selection of other cured meats. But I think this type of cured duck is never better than when served as part of a fresh green salad.

INGREDIENTS

- 1 air-dried and cold-smoked duck breast
- Two handfuls of delicate green salad leaves
- 4 cherry tomatoes (quartered)
- 10 basil leaves
- 4 tsp. balsamic vinegar
- 4 tsp. extra virgin olive oil
- Black pepper

Serves 2

METHOD

1 Place the duck breast fat-side down. With a sharp carving knife cut through the meat at a slight angle to achieve a nice long slice. Cut as thinly as possible.

2 Place a handful of green leaves in the centre of a serving dish and arrange the tomato quarters on and among the leaves.

3 Arrange the duck slices throughout the salad and add the fresh basil leaves as a garnish. To serve, lightly dress with balsamic vinegar and olive oil, adding black pepper to taste.

AIR-DRIED LAMB

Lamb has a distinctive flavour that works superbly with herbs and spices. Air-drying intensifies the flavours, producing a fragrant melt-in-the-mouth delicacy. The technique for curing lamb in this way is not complicated, so give it a try!

KEY STAGES

1 Curing

2 Drying

It is well worth taking the time to try this technique. The result is an unusual and delicious charcuterie product. Although the method is not complicated, air-dried lamb cannot be hurried; drying can take at least three months. So if you intend to cure lamb in this way, be sure to plan ahead. Because curing takes place over a long period, the use of Prague Powder #2 is recommended for safety. A similar method is used to produce prosciutto-style air dried ham (see page 102).

A colourful paprika coating protects the meat while it dries.

YOU WILL NEED
- **2 kg (4½ lb) leg of lamb**

FOR THE CURE
- **100 g (4 oz) salt (plus additional salt to cover the meat during curing)**
- **25 g (1 oz) sugar (optional)**
- **1 tsp. Prague Powder #2**
- **2 tsp. dried rosemary (finely chopped)**
- **1 clove of garlic (crushed)**
- **2 tsp. smoked (or unsmoked) paprika**
- **1 tsp. crushed black peppercorns**
- **White wine vinegar and paprika for drying**

Preparation and Curing

1 Remove as much of the sinew as possible from the inside face of the leg of lamb. Cut away any loose pieces of fat and generally give it a tidy up. Leave the skin in place as it will prevent the meat underneath the fat cap from drying out too much.

2 Mix the cure ingredients together and rub into the flesh of the lamb. Use four fifths of the cure on the flesh side and one fifth of the cure on the skin side. Press the cure into all the little crevices to minimize the risk of spoiling and to ensure even distribution of the flavours.

3 Spread about 1 cm (½ in) of salt in the bottom of a nonreactive container just big enough to fit the meat without it touching the sides. Place the lamb in the container skin side down. Fill the container with enough salt to cover the lamb by about 1 cm (½ in). Place a weight equal to that of the meat on top of the salt layer over the meat.

4 Cure the lamb in the salt for three days for each 1 kg (2¼ lb) of meat plus three days. For example, the 2 kg (4½ lb) leg of lamb specified here needs to cure for nine days.

Drying

1 When the lamb has cured, rinse the leg with cold running water and dry it well with kitchen paper. Rub it down with white wine vinegar. This raises the acidity on the outside of the meat, which encourages helpful bacteria and will help to keep the surface in good condition while air drying. To protect the open surface of the lamb as it is drying, you can apply a layer of paprika, pressing it in so it forms an even coating. This helps protect against flies and other insects and promotes drying by absorbing some of the moisture on the exposed meat surface. It also imparts extra flavour to the meat.

2 Wrap the leg in undyed muslin. Secure with string, label with the date and weight, and hang to air dry for about three months. The texture of the lamb will become firm while retaining a little springiness. Serve in thin slices, perhaps alongside a selection of fine cheeses, or in a green salad with sundried tomatoes with a herb-infused olive oil dressing.

Trim away visible fat and sinew from the surface of the meat.

Place the cure-covered meat on a layer of salt in a nonreactive container.

SAVE ON SALT

Use a container only just big enough to accommodate the meat without it touching the sides. This will save on on space and on the amount of salt you have to use.

AIR-DRIED HAM

Air-dried ham – ham prepared in the style of Italian prosciutto di Parma – is perhaps the most famous of dry-cured meats. This delicately salted delicacy takes upwards of six months to produce and will impress any dinner guest. In Italy these hams are traditionally started as the weather turns cooler in November to help prevent the meat from spoiling in the initial stages before the salt takes effect.

KEY STAGES

1 Preparing

2 Salting

3 Drying

Prosciutto di Parma and Jamón Ibérico (pata negra) are European variations of air-dried ham. Cured in salt and hung to air dry for up to two years, some of these wonderful products have received worldwide acclaim. The pork from which these hams are often made, traditionally comes from pigs reared on a special diet that includes acorns and corn, which are said to affect the flavour of the finished ham.

Managing Large Cuts

Some of the Iberico hams are made using the whole leg including the foot. Curing with the foot on the ham can be a challenge in terms of space, but if you have a large enough curing box to house the complete ham, you can certainly try this out. Otherwise you can ask your butcher to remove the aitch bone and trotter. In the following instructions it is assumed that this has been done. You'll need a large amount of salt to pack the ham in You can buy large quantities of food grade salt online or through wholesale outlets.

Preparing the Meat

1 You will need to massage the ham to remove any unwanted blood that still remains in the femoral artery, which can be found just next to the ball joint of the pork leg. Place the meat on a firm surface and using both hands on the thickest part of the leg massage towards the ball joint until no more blood is seen. Mop up the blood with kitchen paper.

2 Use a sharp knife to remove some of the skin and fat from around the edges of the exposed meat surface of the ham. This allows more of the meat to come into contact with the salt and speeds the curing process. Trim away any loose edges from the exposed meat, so that there will be no straggly bits left when the meat is cured and dried.

Thin curls of air-dried ham are decorative on the plate as well as exquisite to taste (right).

YOU WILL NEED
- **Long-cut leg of pork**

FOR THE CURE
For each 1 kg (2¼ lb) of meat
- **Salt, sufficient to cover the meat plus 250 g (9 oz)**
- **½ tsp. Prague Powder #2**

Making the Cure

1 Weigh the ham and calculate the amount of Prague Powder #2 that you'll need for the size of your ham. You will need to use ½ tsp. of Prague Powder #2 for every 1 kg (2¼ lb) of meat.

2 Mix the Prague Powder with 250 g (9 oz) of salt. Massage four fifths of this mix into the exposed surfaces of the meat paying particular attention to the areas around the ball joint and the joint as the hock end of the ham. Pack these areas really well with salt to prevent spoilage. When you have done this, rub the entire ham with the remaining fifth of the mix.

Curing the Ham

1 The meat is now ready to be salted. You'll need a nonreactive box large enough to house your ham without touching the sides. Pour 25–30 mm (1–1½ in) of salt into the base of the box and spread this around evenly.

2 Place the ham, exposed meat side up, in the box and pour on enough salt to cover the entire ham with a 1-cm (½-in) layer of salt on top. Make sure the salt covers every part of the ham.

3 You will now need to weigh down the ham to assist in removing the moisture from the meat and to ensure a densely textured finished product. Place a wooden board on top of the ham and on top of this place a heavy weight. Aim to use a weight equivalent to that of the ham.

4 Cure the ham in the salt for one and a half days per pound of meat (three days per kilogram) plus two days. During this time keep the ham below 10°C (50°F). When the ham is cured, remove it from the salt and inspect it for spoilage. If it is spoiled, you'll smell it. If this has occurred, don't hesitate to discard it – it won't be safe to eat. Brush off all the salt and wipe the entire ham with a cloth soaked in white wine vinegar.

Prosciutto e Melone

A classic way to serve air-dried ham is as a starter with melon. The Italians call this "prosciutto e melone". The sweetness of a canteloupe melon really works well to offset the saltiness in the air-dried ham. No other ingredients are essential for this simple, summery dish, but you can garnish it with fresh peppery rocket leaves.

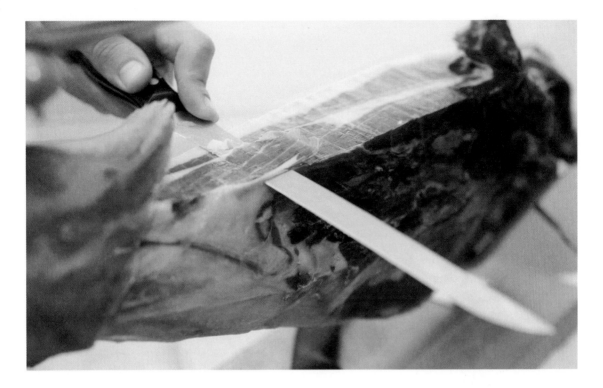

Drying the Ham

1 Wrap the ham loosely in a large piece of undyed muslin and secure with butcher's string. Weigh the ham and label it. Hang in a cool, dry place to air dry. Aim to maintain a temperature of around 15°C (60°F) and a relative humidity of 65 to 75 per cent.

2 When the ham has lost 15–20 per cent of its weight it should be ready to eat. This usually takes around three months. The ham can be allowed to mature for up to two years before it is consumed. When sufficient weight has been lost, to prevent over-drying, mix a blend of plain flour and rendered belly fat with some crushed black peppercorns and apply this to the exposed surfaces of the meat.

Slicing and Serving

To serve, slice the ham very thinly using a sharp, thin-bladed slicing knife (see Slicing and Storing, page 87). Cut a flap of the outside skin away before cutting the ham. This flap of skin can be used to seal the cut surface, which will protect the exposed face of the ham. The exposed surface of the meat can also be covered with clingfilm to prevent it from drying out further.

Air dried hams are traditionally cut on a special mount which will keep the ham firmly in place.

KEEP THE TRIMMINGS

Keep the bones and trimmings from the leg. These can be simmered to make a tasty pork stock. The offcuts and trimmings can also be used for making sausages (see page 115).

PANCETTA

Pancetta is a style of air-dried bacon traditionally made in Italy. Delicately flavoured, it is made from belly pork. It can be rolled or flat and can be used in the same way as bacon or lardons to provide extra flavour to other dishes.

A traditionally rolled pancetta can provide a decorative and delicious starter.

Pancetta looks good as a piece of charcuterie and tastes great on its own, sliced wafer thin, as a starter with a few green leaves. It is made from belly pork, a cut that is ribboned with fat, and it is this fat intermingled with the delicate and aromatic herb blend that gives pancetta its special flavour when cooked.

Versatility

Pancetta is usually cured in herbs and salt, air dried and sometimes cold-smoked with oak (hot smoking would change the character of the meat). Prepared in this way and sliced thinly, pancetta needs no cooking. When sliced more thickly, the meat can be diced into lardons and pan-fried to release its flavours and aromas. When fried, Pancetta lardons can be added to soups, salads, and pasta dishes. This is one of those versatile ingredients I wouldn't want to be without; I always have some in the refrigerator or in a vacuum bag in the freezer ready for use.

Removing the Skin

Pancetta is usually made with the skin removed and just a layer of fat remaining on the outside of the belly. Removing the skin can be a little tricky, so it may be best to ask your local butcher to do this for you. If you decide to do this yourself, make sure that the meat is extremely cold, which makes the process easier. You'll need a sharp knife and a firm board. The technique is similar to that for removing fish skin (see page 128). Try to leave as much fat on the meat as possible as this will protect the meat and stop it from drying out too much.

YOU WILL NEED

- 1 kg (2¼ lb) belly pork

FOR THE CURE
- 1 tbsp. salt
- ½ tsp. Prague Powder #2
- 2 cloves of garlic (crushed)
- 1 tbsp. sugar or honey
- 1 tbsp. crushed black peppercorns
- 1 clove (whole)
- 10 juniper berries (bruised or crushed)
- 2 bay leaves (finely chopped)
- 1 sprig of fresh thyme

FOR THE SEASONING
- 1 tsp. ground nutmeg
- 1 tbsp. crushed black peppercorns

Preparation and Curing

1 Trim the belly pork into an 20-cm (8-in) square and remove the skin, if this has not been done already. Thoroughly mix all the cure ingredients together in a bowl.

2 Apply three quarters of the curing mixture to the exposed meat surfaces of the belly and one quarter to the fat surface. Place the meat in a vacuum bag or sealed plastic bag, and cure in the refrigerator for seven to ten days, turning the bag daily to ensure the mixture is distributed evenly. Remove the pancetta from the bag and rinse in cold water. Pat dry with kitchen paper.

Remove the skin from the belly pork.

Apply the cure mix.

Drying

1 With meat side facing up, firmly press the ground nutmeg and black pepper into the surface of the meat.

2 Roll the pancetta as tightly as possible, making sure there are no air gaps inside the roll. Air gaps can lead to spoilage so take your time with this. Weigh and record the weight of the meat. Pancetta can also be made flat (see Step 3).

3 Tie the meat into a the roll as described on page 110. If you have decided to dry the pancetta unrolled, rub down the whole external surface of the pancetta with white wine vinegar this will cleanse the outside of the meat and increase the acidity, which encourages beneficial yeasts to grow on the surface. If you choose to smoke your pancetta, it should be done at this stage. Read pages 132–157 if you are new to smoking techniques. Cold smoke the pancetta for about eight hours and proceed with the following steps.

4 Wrap the pancetta loosely in undyed muslin and tie it at the top and bottom. Weigh it and leave it to air dry where the temperature is around 15°C (60°F) and the relative humidity is between 65 and 75 per cent. You can also air dry the pancetta in the refrigerator or in dry-aging bags (see page 84).

5 The pancetta will be ready after it has lost 10–15 per cent of its weight, which usually takes three to four weeks if drying naturally. If you intend to serve the pancetta raw in thin slices, aim for a weight loss of 20–25 per cent. When the meat reaches this level of dryness, you should prevent it from losing any more moisture by keeping it wrapped in plastic or vacuum-packed in the refrigerator or freezer.

Roll the meat with the cure inside.

Secure the roll with butcher's knots.

Hang the wrapped meat to dry.

Pancetta Pasta

As well as being a superb element on a charcuterie platter, pancetta is a flavourful addition to many cooked dishes. It works particularly well in a pasta sauce in combination with mushrooms and crème fraîche.

INGREDIENTS

- **125 g (4 oz) pancetta**
- **4 large white mushrooms**
- **1 tsp. butter**
- **1 clove of garlic (crushed)**
- **4 tbsp. olive oil**
- **220 g (8 oz) dried tagliatelli**
- **4 tbsp. crème fraiche**
- **Salt and pepper to taste**
- **2 sprigs of fresh thyme**
- **Parmesan cheese (grated)**

Serves 2

METHOD

1 Dice the pancetta into small cubes and set aside. Slice the mushrooms and set aside.

2 Melt the butter in a very hot frying pan. Stir in the pancetta and fry for five minutes until it develops some colour. Add the garlic and mushrooms and allow to sweat down for a few minutes. Add the olive oil and cook for a further four to five minutes.

3 Meanwhile, cook the tagliatelli in boiling salted water and drain

4 Add the crème fraîche to the pan with the mushooms and pancetta and simmer. Cook for one minute and season to taste. Stir in the cooked pasta with the thyme leaves. Sprinkle with fresh Parmesan cheese to serve.

TYING A PANCETTA

This technique is key to producing a traditionally rolled pancetta. It's a good idea to practise it using a rolled towel before you attempt it with your carefully cured meat.

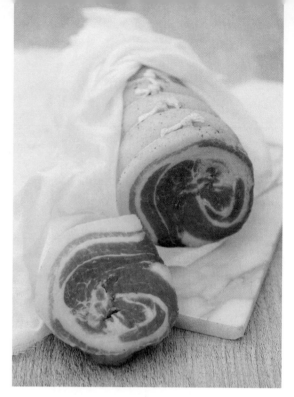

Tie an overhand knot in the running end.

1 With the pancetta neatly rolled, lay butcher's string under the pancetta and tie an overhand knot in the running end of the string.

2 Holding up the standing part (panel, facing page), pass the running end (with the overhand knot) around the standing part leaving yourself enough string to tie a further knot.

3 Holding the running end, tie an overhand knot back on the running end forming a loop around the standing part.

Pass the running and around the standing part.

Tie an overhand knot around the running end.

4 Gently pull on the standing part while holding the running end until the knot closes around the meat. You may need to give the string a bit of a tug to get it to move. When the knot and string is against the meat, tug sharply on the standing part to draw the knot tightly around the pancetta.

5 Make sure the knot is as tight as possible as the pancetta will shrink slightly as it air dries. To lock off this knot, form a loop around the knot.

6 Pull this loop tight around the knot until it sits underneath the previous knot.

7 Trim the knot neatly with a pair of scissors. Secure the rolled pancetta with as many knots tied in this way as you need – as a guide you need to tie knots at about 25-mm (1-in) intervals.

Gently tighten the knot.

Form a loop around the knot.

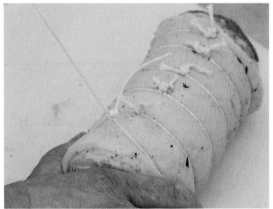

Pull the loop tightly to secure the knot.

A neatly secured roll of pancetta.

KNOT-TYING TERMS

OVERHAND KNOT A simple knot formed by passing the end of the string through a loop in the running end.

RUNNING END The end of the string that does all the work.

STANDING PART The "inactive" part of the string that is still on the roll.

COPPA

Coppa, sometimes called capicola or capocollo, is air-dried pork from the top part of the shoulder of the pig. Cured with pepper, garlic, and fennel, this is a delicacy that will stimulate your taste buds.

KEY STAGES

1 Preparing

2 Curing

3 Seasoning

4 Drying

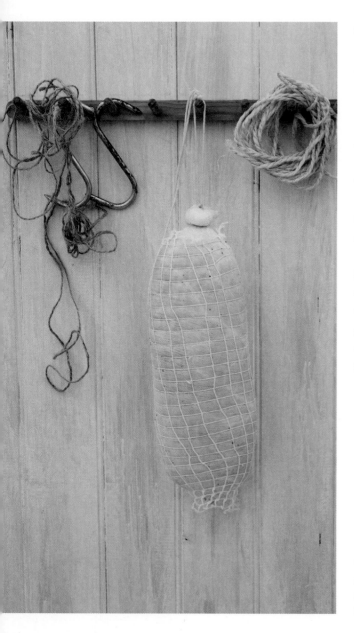

The use of the whole muscle from the collar creates a distinctive-looking piece of charcuterie. This cut is taken from the upper part of the shoulder, sometimes called pork butt or Boston butt. A favourite element of any Italian-style charcuterie board, coppa is very lean and has a firm texture and full flavour, which makes the effort of preparing it worthwhile. It is traditionally stuffed into a natural ox casing (beef bung) to protect it as it dries. It is trussed with butcher's string to keep its shape and to hold the casing close to the meat as it dries.

Slicing and Serving

Coppa is traditionally served as a starter very thinly sliced, often drizzled with olive oil and sprinkled with freshly ground black pepper. Garnish with a few salad leaves and the result is simple, rustic, and delicious.

This homemade coppa is dried in the traditional way in ox casing secured with butcher's netting.

Preparing the Meat

Unless you have a very helpful and knowledgeable butcher, to obtain the correct cut of coppa, you may need to purchase a larger cut from the top of the shoulder and cut the coppa yourself. The collar group of muscles are reasonably easy to remove from the top of a shoulder. Remove the fat from the outside so you just have the muscle group left. There is a little fat between the individual muscles in this group which give coppa its distinctive look.

Curing

1 To cure the meat, use the dredge method, also known as the salt box method. This involves coating the entire surface of the meat in salt by dragging it through salt in a box or dish. This method can be employed for most whole-muscle cured meats. The measurements are a little imprecise but the intention is that you cover the meat with salt in proportion to its size.

2 When the coppa has been coated in salt, place it into a bag along with the other ingredients for the cure. Seal the bag and mix the ingredients around in the bag until the whole muscle is covered in the cure mixture. Weigh the coppa and record this as you'll need this later to judge when it's ready. Cure in the refrigerator for seven days turning the meat daily.

YOU WILL NEED

- **40 cm (15 in) of ox casing (soaked overnight)**

Multiply the following for each 1 kg (2¼ lb) of pork collar in your coppa:

FOR THE CURE
- **2 tbsp. salt**
- **1 tsp. cracked black pepper**
- **5 juniper berries (crushed)**
- **1 clove of garlic (crushed)**
- **½ tsp. Prague Powder #2**

FOR THE SEASONING
- **1 clove of garlic (crushed)**
- **1 tbsp. ground coriander**
- **1 tsp. ground nutmeg**
- **1 tsp. cracked black pepper**

Cover the meat in the cure mix.

Seal in a plastic bag.

Seasoning and Casing

1 Remove the coppa from the refrigerator, rinse it under cold running water, and pat dry with kitchen paper. Combine the seasoning ingredients and apply them evenly to the whole surface of the coppa.

2 Stuff the coppa into the casing, taking care not to tear it. Tie both ends of the casing, secure with butcher's string, and then tie a series of loops around the coppa both lengthwise and around the middle to keep the casing in good contact with the meat. Alternatively, you can use some suitably sized meat netting (see Stuffing the Coppa, below). With a sterile pin, pierce the casing to release any trapped air. Rinse the outside of the whole casing with white wine vinegar.

Drying

Air dry the coppa at around 15°C (60°F) and with a relative humidity of between 65 and 75 for three to four weeks until it becomes firm and the colour darkens. When it is ready, the coppa should have lost about 20 per cent of its original weight. Serve it very thinly sliced.

Insert the seasoned meat into the casing.

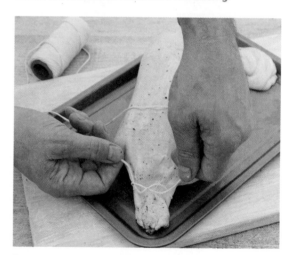

Secure the casing first with a knot close to the end of the coppa.

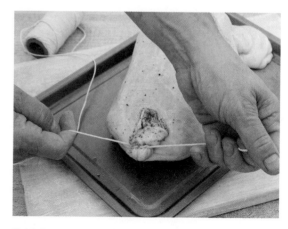

Fold the excess casing over and secure with another knot.

STUFFING THE COPPA

A top tip for getting your coppa to slide inside the meat netting is to use a large plastic bottle (of the type used for fizzy drinks) with a diameter large enough to hold your coppa. Cut off the bottom of the bottle. Pull the net over the neck end of the bottle until it is all gathered near the cut off base.

Insert the coppa into the open base of the bottle until it is almost completely inside. Pull a short length of the net over the base of the bottle and around the end of the coppa. Hold the meat net on the coppa and tilt the bottle so the coppa slides out. As the coppa slides out of the bottle, it will take the meat net with it.

AIR-DRIED CURED SAUSAGES

Making sausages requires some specialized kit and a little bit of time, but the results are worth the effort you need to make to get the basics right. The guidelines here apply to the techniques for classic salami, venison salami, and Spanish chorizo, described on the following pages.

Making any sausage requires the use of a sausage stuffer and casings. Even before you get to that stage, you need to consider how you are going to process the meat; whether you are going to chop the meat by hand or use a mincer, and which cuts of meat you are going to use. The proportions of lean and fat are important when making air-dried cured sausages as these kinds of sausages rarely ever contain rusk or filler that may mask any imbalance.

Safe to Eat Uncooked

The whole point of air-drying sausages is to preserve them so they last a long time or so they can be rendered safe to eat without the need for cooking. Unlike a regular butcher's sausage, which has to be cooked, air-dried sausages are usually cured and dried to the point where they can safely be eaten uncooked.

Casings

Air-dried sausages are usually stuffed into natural casings, which are able to "breathe", allowing moisture through their structure. Some of the newer casings on the market use collagen, which is manufactured from a by-product of meat processing. Collagen casings are thin and strong. Breathable synthetic casings are also available. These are used commercially to produce salami and fermented sausage, but for domestic sausage-makers, these can be difficult to source and are quite expensive.

Fat – A Matter of Texture

Fat plays an important role in sausage-making, especially for the air-dried variety. Some types of pig fat, such as belly fat, have less structure and are used in soft air-dried sausages such as *nduja*, a fermented Italian spreadable salami. This sausage is made with lots of Calabrian red peppers and has a high fat content, mainly belly fat, which has a softer texture than back fat. *Nduja* is stuffed into a natural casing and allowed to dry, but remains spreadable. Back fat is typically used to make salami, black puddings, and chorizo.

Pork fat also plays an important part in the making of sausages from other meats. Venison salami (see page 120), for instance, incorporates pork back fat to provide a firmer texture than that provided by belly fat.

Added Sugar

Sugar or dextrose is used in some fermented sausage recipes. This is not used as a sweetener, but to feed the useful bacteria that add a distinctive acidic flavour to the finished product. These fermented sausages are common in northern Europe and are usually unsmoked. Where smoking is employed, this is limited to cold smoking to preserve the protein structure and therefore the texture of the meat.

CLASSIC SALAMI

A traditionally made, air-dried, fermented sausage, salami originates from Italy. Hung to dry and served in thin slices, this delicacy can be eaten on its own with bread as a snack or as a tasty starter. Making salami is a great project for the novice sausage-maker.

KEY STAGES

1 Mincing

2 Seasoning

3 Stuffing

4 Drying

Salami has a tangy flavour all of its own. This is partly the result of the seasonings used, but is also in part due to the action of the bacteria that help the fermentation process. Salami has a naturally acidity when it's ripe, which is provided by these bacteria. These live cultures digest sugars and produce lactic acid, which inhibits the growth of other, unwanted bacteria. Many recipes also use nitrites (Prague Powder) to prevent the development of dangerous bacteria. But some makers prefer not

to use these, relying purely on the action of helpful bacteria to keep their products safe.

Casings

Salami is stuffed into natural casings where it is hung and allowed to dry naturally in cool breezy conditions. The natural casings allow the moisture to be lost and salami is usually ready when it has lost 25–30 per cent of its initial weight. Salami is usually at least 50 mm (2 in) in diameter, so if you are planning to use natural casings, you'll need to obtain casings of the appropriate size.

Which Cut?

You can use virtually any cut of pork to make salami, but in my opinion a whole shoulder is the ideal cut to use. Skinned and boned out, this cut of meat contains virtually the perfect proportion of fat and lean. If you use a leaner cut of meat, you may need to make up the fat content with additional back fat. Back fat has a firmer texture than belly fat and can be diced to give your finished salami a rustic look, feel, and satisfying texture.

Know the Ratios

The meat/fat ratios for making salami are important to follow. Salami is made from about 80 per cent lean pork meat (usually from the shoulder) and 20 per cent back fat. The fat can either be minced with the meat or it can be diced and put into the mix before the salami is stuffed.

Seasoning Basics

Seasoning and flavouring is a key part of successful salami making. Salami is traditionally seasoned with garlic and pepper, but you can adapt the seasonings to your taste. Be careful not to use too much garlic; this is essentially a raw product so the

garlic taste remains quite strong. Salami can also be flavoured with fennel, paprika, and other aromatics. Traditionalists wouldn't normally smoke this sausage, as this would retard the naturally forming mould bloom on the surface of the casing.

Classic salami is just that – a classic. It is an ever-popular sandwich filler for a picnic or a key element of a mixed charcuterie platter.

YOU WILL NEED
- **1 kg (2¼ lb) pork meat and fat**
- **1 m (3 ft) 50-mm (2-in) diameter natural casings**

FOR THE SEASONING
- **1 tbsp. salt**
- **½ tsp. Prague Powder #2**
- **1 tsp. roasted fennel seeds (crushed)**
- **1 tsp. cracked black pepper**
- **1 clove of garlic (crushed)**
- **2 tbsp. red wine (preferably Italian)**
- **1 tsp. sugar or dextrose powder**

Mincing

1 Dice the lean pork into 25-mm (1-in) chunks in preparation for mincing. Weigh the pork and calculate the amount of fat you require. For every 800 g (1¾ lb) of lean meat you will need 200 g (7 oz) of back fat.

2 Mix the meat and fat together and mince through an 8-mm (⅓-in) plate. This will produce a coarse salami and the fat will be evenly distributed throughout the sausage. If you prefer to see the fat in the salami, you can chop the back fat into 5-mm (¼-in) cubes.

Seasoning

Add all the seasoning ingredients to the minced pork and mix together well for about five minutes. As you do this you will release a muscle protein (myosin) from the pork that acts as a binder and improves the texture of the salami.

Chop the lean pork.

Add the seasoning to the meat mixture.

Mince the meat and fat.

PROTECTING SALAMI

This is an air-dried product, so at some stage you will want to hang the salami outside to allow the breeze to do its work. The challenge here is to stop flies and other determined creatures from getting a free meal. This can be done by keeping the meat in a wire-framed and screened enclosure, where the meat can dry in the air safely, protected from rain and insects.

Stuffing and Drying

1 Pre-soak the casings and load them onto your sausage stuffer. Insert about 1 kg (2¼ lb) of meat mixture into each salami and tie off. Cut off each sausage before starting the next. You can make the sausages smaller if you prefer, but there's something especially grand about a large salami. Each sausage should be about 25 cm (10 in) long. Leave the salami to hang at about 18°C (64°F) for 12 hours.

2 Pierce each casing several times with a sterilized pin to release any trapped air. Weigh the salami and record the weight and date.

3 Hang the salami at a temperature of around 20°C (68°F), or room temperature, for 12 hours to kick start the fermentation. After this stage the salami will be air dried at a lower temperature.

4 Hang in a temperature of around 15°C (60°F) with a relative humidity of between 65 and 75 per cent for three to six weeks until the salami has lost 25–30 per cent of its original weight.

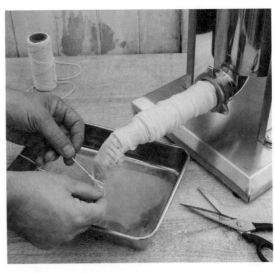

Tie off the end of the casing.

Fill the casing tightly with the sausage mix.

Tie the end of the sausage before starting the next.

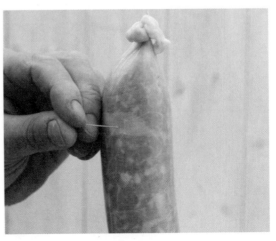

Prick the casing to release any air bubbles.

VENISON SALAMI

Venison salami is a traditionally made, air-dried fermented sausage using a blend of pork and wonderfully rich and lean venison (deer meat). Made using natural casings, this rich-flavoured sausage has to be one of the best salamis you'll taste for a long while.

KEY STAGES

1 Mincing
2 Seasoning
3 Stuffing
4 Drying

Widely used to make a variety of charcuterie delights, venison salami is gaining in popularity in North America and Europe. Venison salami is made using a blend of venison and pork. You can use virtually any cut of venison as it is a very lean meat. The pork fat compensates for the leanness of the venison and also lightens the texture. For venison salami, I use back fat, which has a firmer texture than belly fat. This makes it suitable for dicing.

Lean Meat to Fat Ratios

It is important to follow the meat/pork/fat ratios for making this salami. You need to use about 60 per cent of venison, 20 per cent of lean pork meat, and 20 per cent of pork back fat. The fat can either be minced through with the meat or it can be diced and put into the mix before the salami is stuffed. Venison salami can be seasoned with garlic and pepper, with just a hint of juniper but you can adapt the seasonings to your own taste.

Making Venison Salami

1 Dice the venison and pork into 25-mm (1-in) chunks. Mix the pork and venison together with the fat. Mince and add seasoning as described for classic salami (page 118).

2 Pre-soak the casings and load them onto your sausage stuffer. Insert about 1 kg (2¼ lb) of meat mixture into each salami and tie off. You can make them smaller if you prefer. Venison salami should be no longer than 30 cm (12 in). If it is longer, the salami will distort tapering at the top and bulging at the end, which carries the risk that it will dry unevenly. The ideal length is 20 cm–25 cm (8–10 in).

3 Pierce the casing several times with a sterilized pin to release any trapped air. Leave the salami to hang at about 18°C (64°F) for 12 hours. Continue as described for classic salami (page 118).

Venison salami is a dense, meaty dried sausage that is well worth the effort to produce.

YOU WILL NEED

- **600 g (1¼ lb) venison**
- **200 g (7 oz) lean pork**
- **200 g (7 oz) pork back fat**
- **1 m (3 ft) of 50-mm (2-in) diameter natural casing**

FOR THE SEASONING

- **1 tbsp. salt**
- **½ tsp. Prague Powder #2**
- **5 juniper berries (crushed)**
- **1 tsp. cracked black pepper**
- **1 clove of garlic (crushed)**
- **2 tbsp. Scotch whisky**
- **1 tsp. sugar or dextrose powder**

SPANISH CHORIZO

Chorizo is a spicy Spanish sausage that adds a delicious kick and a rich oiliness to many dishes, including paella, a tomato-based chicken stew, or it can be served as tapas or an antipasto dish. And the good news is that it's surprisingly easy to make.

KEY STAGES

1 Preparation

2 Filling the casings

3 Drying

Spanish chorizo is traditionally secured at both ends to form a ring.

Lovers of Spanish food are likely to be familiar with this flavour-filled, spicy component of every tapas menu and will be excited by the prospect of making this tasty treat at home. This versatile sausage can become a kitchen staple, providing an instant flavour boost to stews and pasta sauces, or an appetite-stimulating snack to accompany pre-dinner drinks.

Fried cubes of chorizo make a crunchy and flavour-rich topping to any vegetable soup.

Preserving Considerations

Chorizo is a pork-based dried sausage, so the basic sausage-making considerations outlined on page 115 apply when making this product. The chorizo made according to the method described here contains 2 per cent salt, which is the normal salinity for a regular butcher's sausage. This air-dried chorizo also contains Prague Powder #2, which is a proprietary blend of salt and sodium nitrite and potassium nitrate. These ingredients are preservatives, which allow for safe air-drying without the risk of bacterial infection. If you decide to use the chorizo straight away in cooking, without a period of drying, you can omit the Prague Powder #2, substituting an additional two teaspoons of salt.

The pork meat for chorizo should ideally come from the shoulder or Boston butt and is 70 to 80 per cent lean to 20 to 30 per cent fat, which is the ideal mix for this sausage. Mince through a 8 mm (^{1}/$_3$ in) plate.

Choosing Casings

Chorizo is made using natural hog casings. The size is a matter of personal choice. The instructions here specify casings of 32–35 mm (1¼–1½ in) diameter. However, bear in mind that chorizo made with larger casings will tend to take longer to dry.

Preparing the Meat

1 Combine the minced pork with the dry ingredients. Add the wine and mix well for about five minutes.

2 Load the meat mix into the sausage stuffer. Using natural hog casings, fill each chorizo with approximately 200 g (7 oz) of meat, and tie both ends together in a ring.

Mix the seasoning and wine into the minced pork.

Drying the Chorizo

1 Prick the casing with a sterilized pin to allow any trapped air to escape and hang the sausage rings to dry in the refrigerator for two weeks.

2 After this time the chorizo can be used in cooked dishes. If you want to use the chorizo as an uncooked starter, leave it to dry for a further two weeks in the refrigerator before serving. Make sure that you weigh and label your chorizo. Aim for a weight loss of around 15 to 20 per cent.

YOU WILL NEED

- **4.3 kg (9½ lb) minced pork**
- **Approximately 4.5 m (15 ft) of 32–35 mm (1¼–1½ in) salted hog casing**

FOR THE SEASONING

- **85 g (3 oz) salt**
- **11.5 g (½ oz) Prague Powder #2**
- **50 g (2 oz) paprika**
- **2 tsp. cayenne pepper**
- **20 g (¾ oz) crushed fennel seeds**
- **50 g (2 oz) minced garlic**
- **200 ml (8 fl oz) red wine (preferably Rioja)**

Prick the casing to release trapped air.

Chorizo Tapas

In Spain tapas dishes are served to accompany wine, but these tasty snacks, often served with crusty bread, can be substantial enough to make a meal. Chorizo is one of the best known tapas.

INGREDIENTS

- **250 g (½ lb) chorizo**
- ½ medium red onion
- 1 tbsp. olive oil
- 2 cloves of garlic
- 2 tbsp. clear honey
- 6 tbsp. red wine
- 1 bay leaf
- Flat-leaf parsley for garnish

METHOD

1 Skin the chorizo and slice into 5-mm (¼-in) thick rounds. Finely slice the red onions. Fry the chorizo in a pan with the olive oil until it begins to release its oil.

2 Add the red onion and garlic. Continue frying until the onions becomes translucent. Add the honey, red wine, and bay leaf, stirring until the honey is dissolved.

3 Reduce the heat and simmer until the liquid reduces by about two thirds and thickens. Serve garnished with chopped parsley.

SALT COD

Enjoyed throughout the Mediterranean and Caribbean, salt cod is easy to produce and is a really lovely way of turning a food with a mild flavour and soft texture into a full-flavoured and distinctively textured delicacy that you can enjoy on its own or as an ingredient in other dishes.

KEY STAGES

1 Salting

2 Drying

Salting is one of the oldest ways of preserving fish and was once the only way to make the catch stretch through lean times. But our ancestors would also have noted salt's impact on the flavour and texture of the fish – just as we do today. Curing cod in dry salt removes a large amount of moisture from the fish rendering it safe to keep for up to three months in the refrigerator or up to a year in the freezer if well wrapped.

Simple Ingredients

To make salt cod, you'll need nothing more than a fresh fillet of cod and salt. You can use sea salt, but ordinary table salt works just well. You could also use PDV (pure dried vacuum) salt (see page 25). You can use just the loin of cod, which is the part of the fillet above the spine, but I prefer to use the whole side. This method works for any reasonable quantity of fish, as long as you have enough space to cure it and enough salt to dry it. You'll need about 250 g (9 oz) of salt for every kilogram (2¼ lb) of fish.

Salt cod look bland, but it provides a unique flavour and texture.

Choose good quality, fresh cod fillets for this product.

COD ALTERNATIVES

Over the past 30 years or so, many of the North Atlantic cod fisheries have been closed or subjected to strict quotas in response to the sharp decline in stocks. While cod is still widely available, it is possible to use other white fish to produce the similar results. Alternatives to cod include haddock, coley, and pollock.

Preparing the Fish

1 First remove the skin from the cod fillet. Your fishmonger can do this for you but it's reasonably easy to do yourself. Lay the fish flat on a chopping board, skin side down. Holding the knife flat on the board, cut horizontally into the fillet just above the skin. Move the knife back and forth, keeping the blade as flat as possible and as close to the skin as you can.

2 When you are able to see the skin separated from the flesh, hold the skin with one hand while moving the knife back and forth with the other in a sawing motion, taking care not to cut through the skin itself. Pull the skin in the opposite direction to that of the cut. Continue this process until all the skin is removed.

Salting

1 Pour half the salt into the base of a nonreactive dish and then add the fish. Coat the fish on both sides with the salt and then add the remaining salt on top of the fish. If you are salting more than one piece of cod in the same dish, separate the pieces by salt in layers so the second layer of fish can be placed on top of the layer of salt above the first fillet and so on for the total number of fillets you will be using.

2 When you've covered the last fillet in salt, cover the dish with clingfilm and allow the fish to cure in the refrigerator for one day for every 25 mm (1 in) of thickness. This measurement the individual thickness of each fillet and not the total thickness if you are using more than one piece. Remove the fish after this time. It is now ready for use.

Cut into the fillet above the skin.

Cover the fish in salt.

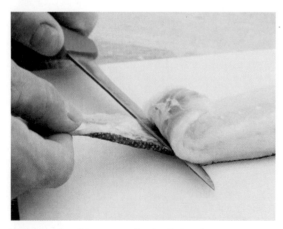

Holding the skin, move the knife back and forth.

Remove the fish from the salt when the curing time has elapsed.

Salt Cod and Tomatoes

This combination of salt cod, tomatoes, garlic, and red peppers is heart-warming dish often prepared during the festive season in Spain. This recipe takes a little over half an hour to prepare and cook, but the salt cod needs to be soaked for at least 24 hours before it is ready to use.

INGREDIENTS

- 1 kg (2¼ lb) salt cod
- 1 large onion (chopped)
- 4 cloves of garlic (roughly chopped)
- 800 g (28 oz) tinned chopped tomatoes
- 4 large roasted red peppers
- 10 black olives (pitted)
- 1 bay leaf
- 1 small sprig of thyme
- 125 g (4 oz) plain flour
- 100 ml (4 fl oz) olive oil

Serves 6

METHOD

1 Soak the cod in cold water for 24 hours, changing the water every eight hours. Remove the cod from its soaking water and pat dry with kitchen paper.

2 Liberally coat the cod with the flour. Heat the olive oil in a large frying pan. Add the cod and lightly fry until just golden. Remove from the pan and set to one side.

3 Add the chopped onion and garlic and fry on a medium heat until translucent. Add the chopped tomatoes, bay leaf, and thyme and stir. Reduce the heat and allow to simmer for about 15 minutes.

4 Return the cod to the pan. Add the roasted red peppers and olives, and simmer gently for another five to ten minutes. Serve with boiled potatoes.

Smoking Meat and Fish

INTRODUCTION TO HOT AND COLD SMOKING

This chapter opens up the world of food smoking and explains how and why we smoke food and how smoking works. For the beginner this part of the book provides pointers for choosing equipment to enable you to undertake this artisan craft at home, with step-by-step instructions on how to construct smokers from easily available materials. The chapter is packed with information about food smoking techniques, for example, for making your own smoked salmon and smoked spare ribs.

Whether you are considering hot or cold smoking, it's worth reflecting for a moment to wonder where or when we actually decided the flavour of smoke on our food was something we liked. Our prehistoric ancestors would have kept themselves warm and cooked on open fires, using indigenous local wood. It's logical to assume that their food would have been coated in the residue from the smoke and thus this wood smoke

seasoning would have been an integral flavour in the food eventually becoming a part of our food heritage. It's safe to assume that ancient humans noticed food that had a light coating of wood smoke residue lasted longer than untreated meat – a fact that scientists examining the properties of

Small chickens can be hot smoked in a stove-top improvised smoker.

HOT OR COLD SMOKING – WHICH TO CHOOSE?

Hot smoking includes a cooking process that can last for several hours. This is not part of the cold smoking process, which preserves the food without altering its texture. Generally hot-smoked products can be eaten straight from the smoker with no further cooking. Most cold-smoked foods require further cooking before being eaten, but there are some exceptions to this rule. The table (right) lists the common cold-smoked foods that require further cooking and those that do not.

wood smoke have only confirmed in the recent past. That smoked food lasts longer and tastes great is no surprise to those who love it and in many ways explains why this flavouring technique has stood the test of time.

Smoked Food Today

The application of smoke to food has been adopted widely throughout the world to add flavour and character to myriad different ingredients. There are two main methods of adding smoke to food. One method requires no addition of heat; the smoke is cool enough not to change the nature of the food while imparting the wonderful flavour of wood smoke. Cold smoking gives flavour to foods like salmon, cheese, and some vegetables.

The other method is hot smoking, which, in its simplest form, is cooking food in the presence of smoke. When hot smoking, the food is cooked while the food is in a smoky atmosphere. Some of the techniques used to hot smoke operate at what are considered to be low cooking temperatures and use extended cooking times in the presence of smoke. Both hot and cold smoking produce wonderfully succulent results, preserving and developing the character and flavour of the meat

FURTHER PREPARATION OF COLD-SMOKED FOODS

Refer to this chart to find out which cold-smoked foods require additional cooking.

READY TO EAT	REQUIRES COOKING
Air-dried duck	Bacon
Salmon (cured)	Beef
Sausage (cured/air dried)	Chicken
	Cod
Trout (cured)	Duck
Tuna (cured)	Goose
Virginia ham	Haddock
	Ham
	Kippers
	Mackerel
	Pheasant
	Rabbit
	Sausage
	Tuna
	Turkey
	Venison

or fish. Hot smoking is widely used as a staple among the barbecue enthusiasts and has a healthy and growing popularity. Many smoked products are well known. Delicacies like Scottish-style smoked salmon, smoked mackerel, smoked duck breasts, and pastrami are but a few of the many popular smoked foods that are widely available in good delicatessens and restaurants.

HOW SMOKING WORKS

In its simplest form, smoking involves the application of smoke residue onto food. But an understanding of the key differences between hot and cold smoking is essential knowledge for anyone considering trying this method of preserving and flavouring food.

Smoking can be done either in a hot environment in which the food is cooked at the same time (hot smoking) or it can be done at much lower temperatures, in which the food remains raw or cured (cold smoking). Both these methods add flavour to the food but only hot smoking cooks the food so it can be eaten immediately. Most cold smoked foods require further cooking to make them safe to eat. But there are a few exceptions to this rule including vegetables, cheeses, and Scottish-style smoked salmon.

What is Wood Smoke?

When considering how smoking works, it's worth spending a little time exploring exactly what smoke is, or to be precise, what wood smoke is. In essence, wood smoke is a product of combustion and it contains many complex and interesting chemical compounds. Some of these chemicals are good for us and some are less so. When wood is heated in a fire it releases lots of compounds into the smoke that is produced, including carbon monoxide (CO), which is a poisonous gas, water vapour, carbon dioxide (CO_2), and many phenolic compounds. There are of course other substances that give wood smoke its characteristic aroma and flavour. These are heavier compounds and they condense onto the food imparting colour, flavour, and aroma.

In days gone by we relied on these compounds in the wood smoke to preserve food as there was no refrigeration other than seasonal cold weather to keep our food from spoiling. Nowadays, since we can keep our food chilled in the refrigerator, wood smoke is used primarily as flavouring.

Making Smoke

We've leaned what's in smoke, but how is it produced? Making smoke is a complex subject in its own right. Here we will focus on the broad principles of making smoke. Simply put, when wood is heated to between 200°C (390°F) and 300°C (570°F), it will start to break down. What we see as smoke is this process of fragmentation in action. The smoke is a mixture of chemicals produced in the course of the reaction when the wood is heated. Smoke is a vapour that can be fragrant and flavour-enhancing in low concentrations on our food, but is nevertheless a respiratory irritant that we should avoid inhaling.

Fish hung in a smoker are exposed to a variety of substances in the smoke that provide flavour and aroma.

The Triangle of Fire

We know that wood burns when it is heated. This process can be visualized by means of the Triangle of Fire (see below). The triangle is made up of three sides: oxygen (usually in the surrounding air), heat (from the source of ignition), and fuel (the wood used to create the smoke).

When all three of these sides are in balance, fire and heat are produced in abundance. When we want to generate smoke, we don't necessarily want fire and heat. To achieve this, we need to adjust the relationship between the sides of the triangle. You can slow down the reaction by reducing the amount of oxygen available so that there is less heat and more smoke. But if you reduce the oxygen too much, the whole process grinds to a halt.

The Right Fuel

Wood dust under the right conditions will smoulder to produce lots of smoke and little heat – ideal for cold smoking. We also know that wood chips or chunks are less likely to smoulder by themselves and will self-extinguish. It is possible to get chips to smoulder with the assistance of an air draft. There is more information about improvised and purpose-made smoke generators later in this chapter.

The Pre-Curing Stage

For some foods such as fish and some meats, there is usually a pre-curing stage, which is essential in the overall smoking process. This stage adds flavour and makes the food less liable to spoil when undergoing the sometimes time-consuming process of smoking. Pre-curing usually involves the application of salt for a period of time. This alters the flavour and texture of the food as well as enhancing the flavour of the smoke. Salt can be applied either as dry salt or in the form of a liquid brine, which can be as simple as salt and water. The use of salt in the curing of food is discussed in depth on pages 14–29.

THE TRIANGLE OF FIRE

The triangle of fire diagram shows the elements required for the combustion process. If any one of these elements is removed or restricted, combustion will slow down or even cease. In food smoking the aim is to maintain this process at the point at which the combustion process is on the point of going out, which is when the maximum amount of smoke is created and heat levels are low.

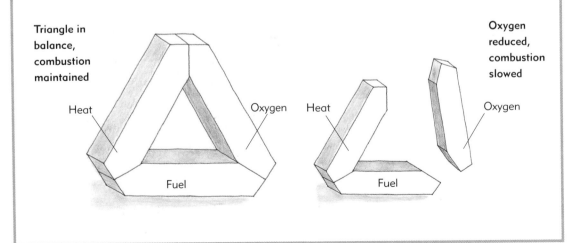

Triangle in balance, combustion maintained

Heat

Oxygen

Fuel

Oxygen reduced, combustion slowed

Heat

Oxygen

Fuel

EQUIPMENT YOU WILL NEED

To smoke food, you will need certain items of equipment. What you need will depend on the type of smoking you are planning to undertake, but some items are common to both hot and cold smoking.

For the purposes of this book, the assumption is that you will already have certain basic items of kitchen equipment including weighing scales, bowls and pans, barbecue tongs, and a good selection of cook's knives, forks, and other utensils. In addition, you will need the items of specialist smoking equipment listed here.

A Smoker

For cold smoking this can be a simple homemade cardboard or wooden smoker (see pages 140–147), or a top of the range purpose-built smoker (see page 142) that can be used for both hot and cold smoking. For hot smoking, you can improvise with a pair of roasting trays (see page 151), use a purpose-made stovetop smoker, or adapt your outdoor barbecue grill (see page 148). For details of suppliers, see the Resources section at the end of the book.

Smoke Generator

A purpose-built smoker of the type pictured on page 139 incorporates a built-in smoke generator. For other types of smoking setup you will need a separate smoke generator. In a basic smoker this may be simply a foil packet enclosing a small quantity of wood chips (see page 149). But for a more substantial setup, you may choose to buy a smoke generator. You can choose from a simple burn tray, a maze-type burn tray, an air-driven smoke generator, through to an electrical heat pad and a friction-based smoke generator. The main consideration in choosing a smoke generator suitable for your needs comes down to the type of smoking you are looking to do. It's true that it is possible to use all the smoke generators described

here for hot smoking, but to gain successful results using a smoke generator that incorporates a heat source, you will need to separate the heat from the smoke. You'll find further advice on choosing the right kind of smoke generator for your needs in the section on Understanding Your Smoker, page 138.

Wood Chips and Wood Dust

There are several varieties of commercially produced wood chips and wood dust on the market and many suppliers stock a wide range of barbecue smoking chips. Wood dust is used primarily for cold smoking because it tends to smoulder and produces quite low levels of heat. Wood chips burn at a higher heat and are used for hot smoking. For more information on the characteristics of different types of wood and wood products, see page 154.

Digital Thermometer

This is used to check the temperature inside the smoker to ensure that the food has been smoked at the correct temperature for food safety.

Food Racks

When smoking food, it is always a good idea to place it on something that is food safe and easy to clean. I use chromed or stainless steel food racks for my smoking. These can be cleaned in a dishwasher after use to keep them clean and hygienic. Food racks of this type can be purchased from any good kitchen supply shop.

Water Spray Bottle

This is a useful item if you are going to smoke food on the barbecue. It can be filled with clean water and used to suppress a flare up. Use of a spray will

KEY

1 Large burn tray

2 Large maze-style smoke generator

3 Chef's smoke gun

4 Smoke generator tin

5 Small maze-style smoke generator

6 Foil package smoke generator

also add a little moisture to the wood chips when they are on the charcoal, helping your food to remain moist.

Duct Tape

This versatile and sturdy tape can be used to join pieces of equipment together and I use it to seal the top of my cardboard smoker when it's running. But be aware that it is not food safe so keep it away from contact with food, and also from heat and fire.

Hygiene Equipment

If you are going to handle food, it's worth investing in some basic hygiene equipment. Disposable gloves, hand sanitizer (antibacterial hand wash and antibacterial hand gel), and kitchen paper are a good start. I also recommend a full-length apron. All the advice given under Safety and Hygiene (page 30) applies to the food preparation techniques described in this chapter.

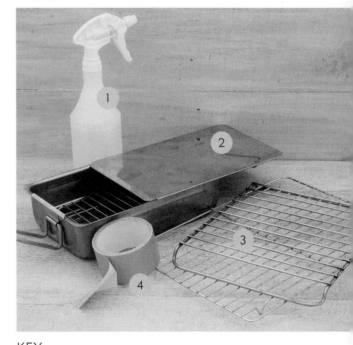

KEY

1 Water spray bottle

2 Stovetop smoker

3 Food racks

4 Duct tape

UNDERSTANDING YOUR SMOKER

Here focus is on the basics and broad principles of hot and cold food smoking. On these pages you'll learn about the parts of the smoker that are important in achieving your desired results.

A smoke generator can be either a self-sustaining smouldering wood dust type or it can be a mechanically sustained smoke generator, which requires the addition of a means of supplying an artificial draft to assist in maintaining the smoulder. These can combust wood chips and chunks successfully. A further category of smoke generators are simply fire pits or charcoal burners (such as a barbecue). In these setups the wood chips are either in direct contact with the coals or are indirectly heated using a foil package or a metal wood chip container (see page 137).

Some smoke generators, such as those using wood dust, are more suited to cold smoking as they produce extremely low levels of heat. Smoking by means of a fire pit or charcoal-driven smoke generator is often more suited to hot smoking as there is usually enough heat to assist in the cooking process too. However, charcoal-driven smoke generators can also be used for cold smoking, providing you are able to separate the smoke from the heat. Some generators use electrical power to ignite the wood thereby generating smoke.

Smoking Compartment

The smoking compartment is simply the area where the food is placed during smoking and that holds the smoke in contact with the food for long enough to allow it to impart it's wonderful flavour. This can be as sophisticated as a stainless steel cabinet specifically designed for smoking food or it can be as simple as a converted cardboard box (see page 144). Some smokers – usually hot smokers

– have the burner or heat source in the smoking compartment with the food, while others – usually cold smokers – use a remote smoke source to carry the smoke into the smoking compartment through a pipe (see page 142). But where the smoke source provides little heat, it can be located in the same compartment as the food even when you are cold smoking. A water pan is a useful addition, especially for hot smoking, where there is a risk that the meat or fish could become too dry.

Fuel Burner

The fuel burner, or heat source, can be natural gas, propane, or electrically driven, or it may be a charcoal-fuelled barbecue or a fire pit. In hot smoking setups, the burner generates the smoke and also provides heat to cook the food while it smokes. Many purpose-built smokers have a separate smoke generator and oven heat source. This makes this type of smoker equally suitable for both hot and cold smoking. Although the smoker pictured on the facing page has a separate smoke generator, it is located within the smoking cabinet. There is an additional attachment for cold smoking that allows the smoke generator to be separated from the cabinet, enabling the smoke to be carried into the smoker at a lower temperature.

Smoke Pipe

A smoke pipe is used when there is a need to generate smoke in a separate location away from the smoking compartment. This can be for a variety of reasons such as the layout of your equipment or the type of equipment you are using. Another reason for using a smoke pipe is when you need to separate the heat from the smoke. This can be particularly important when cold smoking. Using a heat source or fire pit to generate the smoke can produce large quantities of heat, which is not helpful if you are trying to maintain low temperatures within the smoking cabinet. The smoke pipe can be used to cool the smoke before it enters the smoking compartment. If this is your aim, the pipe can either be buried or exposed to the air, allowing excess heat to dissipate.

Damper

In some smokers that have a remote smoke source or in those that are fed from a fire pit, there can be a danger of creating a "draw", when the excess air feeding the fire pit could cause the smoke to overheat and, in extreme cases, catch fire. A draw is caused primarily by the warmed smoke rising through a smoke pipe. A damper is used to check this process and control the speed at which the smoke travels. Some smokers have a vent in the top, which is sometimes referred to as a passive damper, as it is not adjustable.

Other Features

Most commercial food smokers have a means of gauging the temperature inside it – a useful feature for both cold and hot smoking. Sophisticated models may have thermostatically controlled heating elements that can adjust the temperature inside the smoker. Smokers designed for commercial use may have fully automatic, mechanically fed electrical smoke generators with humidity controls, electrostatic filters to control emissions, and computer assistance to ensure consistency of conditions. But such automation is not feasible for most home smokers.

A top-of-the-range home smoker is pictured here. It incorporates all the main features mentioned on these pages, but you can also improvise these functions in a home-built smoker (see pages 140–151).

KEY

1 Damper/vent
2 Food racks
3 Fuel feeder tube
4 Door
5 Smoke generator
6 Drip tray
7 Water dish
8 Heating element
9 Fuel burner
10 Drip bowl/ash pan
11 Bottom tray

IMPROVISING A COLD SMOKER

Building your own cold smoker can be a hugely rewarding experience. The possibility of having the right equipment to be able to create delicious food in your own home without the expense of buying a purpose-built smoker is just the motivation you need to have a go at making a cold smoker yourself.

A home cold-smoker can be as simple or as elaborate as you like. Providing you follow a few simple rules you won't go far wrong.

The Essentials of a Smoker

To build your own smoker you need to think of it in very simple terms. A smoker is in essence a container that keeps the smoke in the same environment as the food. Whether you intend to build a wooden cold smoker or use a converted oil drum or a filing cabinet (providing they have been cleaned to remove any oils), making your own cold smoker should be well within your capabilities.

Get the Size Right

It's essential to consider the size of the food racks you'll be using when designing your smoker so that they fit into the smoking compartment. I designed my food smoker (pictured on the facing page) so it would be large enough to fit racks that would support a whole side of salmon. You may want to consider the possibility of making a stacking smoker, which is useful when you have lots to smoke or hang. In this design modular smoking compartments are placed one on top of the other. The size can be reduced to one stacking module when you only have a few items to smoke.

TEA-LIGHT SMOKER

The tea-light cold smoker is a simple tabletop arrangement that uses the heat from two small tea lights to combust wood chips or dust to produce smoke. The smoker is made from two metal boxes: the smoking compartment and the fire box. These are separated by an air gap but linked by a short ducting. The tea lights provide enough heat to produce smoke for about three hours.

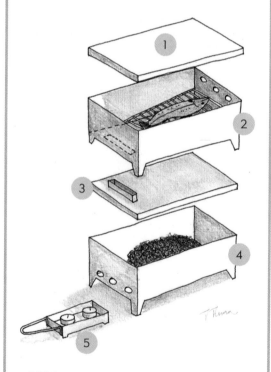

KEY

1 Smoking compartment lid
2 Smoking compartment with food rack
3 Fire box lid with duct for smoke
4 Fire box
5 Tea-light burner tray

This simple but effective wooden cold smoker was constructed by hand and produces excellent results.

FILING CABINET SMOKER

An old metal filing cabinet can make a very effective improvised cold smoker. Just cut a hole in the top for a damper/vent, insert one or more food racks in the upper drawers, and place a small smoke generator in the bottom drawer.

KEY

1 Damper/vent

2 Drawer converted to hold a food rack

3 Bottom drawer to hold smoke generator

Ensure Easy Access

Design your smoker so that you can easily gain access to your food during and after smoking by including a close-fitting door with a snug seal around it to prevent smoke escaping. Some smokers designed for food to be hung inside have an access lid on the top of the smoker through which the food can be lowered.

Consider Smoke Production

Think about the way you intend to generate smoke. If you intend to house a small smoke generator for cold smoking within the smoker, you'll need to carry out some simple experiments to assess how much additional heat this will generate when in operation. A small generator may add an additional 2°C (4°F) to a small volume smoker (0.2 cu m/8 cu ft). The larger the smoker, the more smoke you will need from your generator. A small generator can produce enough smoke for a smoker up to about 0.5 cu m (16 cu ft.). There are large burn trays available for larger smokers.

Choose a Ducting

If you need to generate your smoke remotely and duct it into the smoker then you may need to find a flexible ducting that fits the purpose. Light gauge aluminium ducting is readily available in various diameters and is ideal for transmitting smoke from the source of the smoke into the smoker. Do not use duct tape on this pipe unless you can guarantee the pipe will not get too hot.

Design the Height of Smoker and Smoke Source

If you are considering using a remote smoke pipe, give some thought to the height of the smoker above the smoke source. If the height is too great, the draw caused by the rising warm smoke could cause a flare up in the smoke source, sending more heat and less smoke up the pipe. Aim for a short height difference that produces a gentle draw.

A Separate Fire Box?

If you are using a smoke generator inside the smoker, it can be an advantage to create a separate fire box below the smoking compartment. This saves you from having to open the door to the smoker when checking on the smoke production. Using a flexible pipe is a good way of separating the heat from the smoke when cold smoking.

Incorporate a Damper

Part of the process of cold smoking is to allow the food to continue to dry a little while it receives the smoke. To allow moisture to leave the smoker,

USING A REMOTE SMOKE SOURCE

The setup shown here is for a cold smoker with a remote smoke source.
The length of the smoke pipe ensures that excess heat in the smoke is dissipated
before it comes into contact with the food inside the smoker.

1 Air enters the fire box and the wood combusts to create smoke and heat.

2 The smoke pipe transmits the smoke to the smoker. Some of the heat produced with the smoke is lost through the pipe.

3 Cooled smoke enters the smoker.

4 The food inside the smoker is exposed to cool smoke, which improves flavour and aids preservation but does not cook the food.

a small opening at the top of the smoker is required. This is called the damper, or vent, and if you are using a remote smoke pipe to send the smoke into the smoker this hole needs to be controlled or partially covered. When a smoker is fitted with a damper at the top, the smoke will escape slowly and eventually the balance of smoke being produced against the smoke being lost will cause the level of smoke in the smoker to become stable.

Spread the Smoke

A smoke spreader is a device that spreads the smoke evenly around the whole surface area of the smoker to make sure everything inside the smoker gets a good dose of smoke. Smoke spreaders are generally used in larger smokers to ensure even smoke coverage. Incorporating a diffuser or smoke spreader in your improvised smoker will help to ensure that the smoke spreads throughout the smoker as it rises (see below). This is particularly important if you are considering making a large smoker.

WHY SPREAD THE SMOKE?

A smoke spreader, which is essentially a piece of metal (or even foil) with holes in it, is designed to sit in between the source of the smoke and the smoker cabinet. It ensures that the smoke mushrooms out at a lower level and then rises evenly through the smoker.

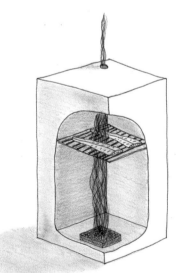

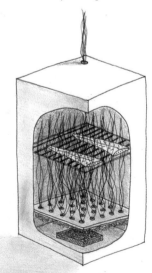

In a smoker without a smoke spreader, the smoke rises in a straight column through the smoker so that the food on the racks is unevenly exposed to the smoke.

In a smoker with a smoke spreader fitted, the smoke rises across the whole surface area of the smoker, so that all the food is exposed evenly to the smoke.

MAKING A CARDBOARD SMOKER

A cold smoker made from cardboard may be the ultimate in low-impact re-use of resources. Simple-to-construct, this improvised cold smoker can turn out some of the best smoked food you're ever likely to taste.

The cardboard smoker uses a small smoke generator that smoulders wood dust on a metal tray to create the smoke. Wooden dowels are passed through holes in the side of the cardboard box and support the food racks in the upper part of the box. You need a small hole in the top of the box to encourage the flow of smoke and a small access flap at the bottom of the box to provide access to the smoke generator. Then all you have to do is place your meat or fish in the box, close the lid, light the generator, and you're well on the way to sampling the delights of smoked food.

SIZE MATTERS

The box should ideally be approximately 60 cm (600 mm/24 in) in height, length, and depth. But these are just guidelines and there is no need to be exact.

YOU WILL NEED
- **A large square box of good-quality, clean cardboard**
- **2 wire food racks (see Constuction Tips, page 147)**
- **2.4 m x 9 mm (8 ft x ³/₈ in) hardwood dowel cut into 60-cm (600-mm/24-in) lengths.**
- **Duct tape**
- **Sharp craft knife**

Making the Base and Lid

1 Many shop-bought cardboard boxes are sold "flat". First form the box by closing the base and taping it closed with a small strip of duct tape.

Close the base of the box with duct tape.

2 Cut down the two inner flaps at the top of the box to about 50 mm (2 in). This is important as they are likely to sag touching the food if left uncut. Make sure you cut only the inner flaps. If you cut the outer flaps you won't be able to close the smoker.

Cutting the Dowel Holes

1 Mark the positions of the dowel holes on each side of the box using a food rack as a guide. Ensure you make these as horizontal as you can. Mark the first pair of dowel holes 100 mm (4 in) from the top of the box; mark second pair of dowel holes 100 mm (4 in) lower.

2 Pierce the holes for the dowels. Reinforce the holes with a square of duct tape. Make a small hole in the duct tape using the scissors and insert a length of dowel.

3 In one of the narrow sides of the box, cut a flap large enough to access the smoke generator plus the tray it sits on, and reinforce the edges using duct tape.

Cut down the inner flaps of the top of the box.

Mark the dowel positions.

Reinforce the holes with tape.

Cut a flap in one of the narrow sides.

Creating the Smoke Duct Hole

1 In the centre of the opposite side of the box, mark and cut a 100-mm (4-in) circular hole about 50 mm (2 in) from the bottom of the box and reinforce this opening with duct tape. This hole is to allow you to supply smoke from a remote source through a pipe or duct. Keep the cut-out circle of card, as this will be used on the roof of the smoker to cover the damper.

2 Cut out a 125 x 150-mm (5 x 6-in) rectangle of cardboard from one of the discarded flaps and reinforce the edges with duct tape. Use duct tape to attach this piece of cardboard above the circular hole cut in Step 1. This flap will cover the hole when the smoke pipe is not in use.

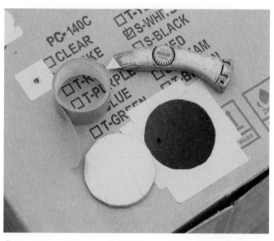

Cut and reinforce a hole in the side of the box.

Make a flap to cover the hole.

Making the Damper

1 Make a 75-mm (3-in) circular hole in one of the roof flaps. This will act as the ventilation hole (or damper) when using a remote smoke pipe. Reinforce the sides of the hole with duct tape.

2 Reinforce the card retained from the smoke-pipe hole with duct tape and staple this over the hole in the roof to enable you to adjust the size of the vent, which will control the draw when operating from a remote smoke source.

Cut a hole in the top flap for the damper.

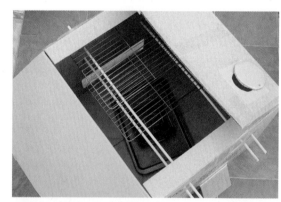

Staple a circle of card over the hole to create an adjustable cover.

BE SAFE

Cardboard will catch fire if it comes into contact with smouldering wood dust. Always place the smoke generator inside the smoker on a non-combustible (preferably metal) tray. Never use a naked flame in or near this type of smoker. This smoker is only to be used as a cold smoker.

CONSTRUCTION TIPS

• Check the wire racks you have selected to support your food during smoking against your box to make sure they fit. You should be able to fit two racks side by side in a large box.

• Make sure the dowels are horizontal. If they are at an angle, there is a risk that your food will slide or roll off the rack when placed in the smoker.

• When measuring the position of the holes for the dowels, use one of the flaps that have been cut off as a template. This will help ensure that position of the holes is the same on both sides.

USING A CARDBOARD SMOKER

A cardboard smoker should be used with a maze-type smoke generator that burns fine wood dust. The generator should be placed on a metal tray to protect the cardboard beneath.

Remote Smoke Considerations

If you connect a remote smoke source to your cardboard smoker via a pipe, try to avoid placing the pipe too vertically; this will create too much of a draw and therefore too much heat in the smoker. Remember that the ventilation hole (damper) on the top of the smoker can be used to control the draw in the pipe and to balance the smoke generation. If the smoker becomes too hot, you can partially close the hole to restrict oxygen supply and reduce heat production.

CHOICE OF SMOKER

With a cardboard smoker you have a choice of either using a small smoke generator inside the smoker itself (5) or, alternatively, using a separate smoke pipe with a remote fire box smoke generator (8). Both are shown in the drawing for illustration purposes, but you only need to choose one.

KEY

1 Damper
2 Food racks
3 Wooden dowels
4 Access flap
5 Small burn tray-type smoke generator in metal tray
6 Hole for alternative smoke supply
7 Smoke pipe
8 Remote fire box smoke generator

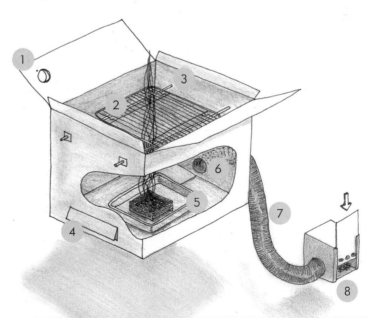

IMPROVISING A HOT SMOKER

Making your own hot smoker can be an effective way to start smoking your own food and will deliver excellent results. This can be done using a few items of everyday kitchen equipment and won't cost you much.

A hot smoker can be improvised using a charcoal barbecue grill. Some barbecues don't have a lid and if you've constructed your barbecue from bricks or stones then you probably won't have a lid. A lidless barbecue can be adapted for smoking small cuts such as chicken pieces, steaks or lamb chops, but can also be used to smoke larger cuts such as a whole lamb shoulder.

Most barbecues these days come complete with a purpose-made lid. If you have one of these, then you already have a ready-made hot smoker.

Enclosing Your Barbecue

To smoke on a barbecue without a lid it's necessary to create an enclosure that can sit over the food to keep the smoke in contact with the food. This can be done in a variety of ways. You can place an upturned roasting tray over the food on the barbecue to prevent the smoke escaping while the food is cooking. Although this method provides only a small enclosure to contain the smoke, it can produce great end results. See the instructions on the facing page.

Alternatively, you can use aluminium foil to construct a rudimentary cover to enclose the food cooking on the barbecue. I have used this method on a portable barbecue to make the most wonderful Hickory smoked chicken.

Some stone or brick-built garden barbecues have adjustable shelf fittings to allow you to move the grill plate up or down to vary the distance between the food and the coals. This is a useful feature as the back and sides of the barbecue have a surround

that can be used to help keep the smoke in contact with the food in combination with a sheet of steel or perhaps a spare grill covered in foil.

Choosing the Right Smoking Medium

In order to smoke food on a barbecue you will first have to decide on how you are going to generate smoke. Wood chips or chunks are the usual choice as the smoking medium for barbecues. This is because chips burn slowly and chunks burn even

A barbecue with a lid can be a ready-made smoker.

slower and can produce smoke for up to an hour. Wood dust on the other hand burns far too quickly to achieve effective results.

It is best to apply the wood chips (or chunks) directly on top of the charcoal. It is good practice to put the wood chips to one side of the area in which the food is to be placed in case of a flare up.

Preventing Flare-Ups

A useful tip for suppressing flare-ups is to make sure that the wood chips are a little damp (see Tips, page 150). Another method is to place the wood chips into a small foil packet (see below). This will still allow the heat from the charcoal to cause the wood to smoulder and generate smoke while the foil will prevent the wood chips from flaring up.

Making a Foil Smoke Generator

1 Place a handful of wood chips in the middle of a piece of aluminium foil approximately 30 cm (12 in) square.

2 Fold the edge of the foil approximately one third across. Then fold over the other loose edge of foil sealing in the wood chips.

3 Lightly press down on the foil package at the edges to ensure all the wood chips are in the centre of the package. Fold over the remaining two ends of the foil package to the centre forming a tight package.

4 Turn the package over so the folds are on the bottom. Pierce small holes in the top to allow the smoke to be released from the package when it's heated directly on the barbecue.

Fold the foil over the woodchips.

Fold the ends into the centre to form a package.

Pierce holes in the foil package.

TIPS

• Soaking the wood chips in water can prevent flare-ups and lengthen the time the chips produce smoke. It's recommended that you soak wood chips in water for about an hour, drain them completely, and then lightly sprinkle them on the charcoal.

• When using an upturned roasting dish, you may need to reduce the cooking time a little. This is because this method not only traps the smoke but also concentrates the heat.

• Be sure to use appropriate safety equipment when handling hot items on a barbecue.

From Barbecue to Hot Smoker

1 Place the foil package hole side uppermost directly onto hot charcoal. After a few minutes the heat will act on the wood chips to create smoke. Replace the grill. Place the food on the grill.

2 Place an upturned metal roasting tray over the food when the food is about 50 per cent done. The meat or fish can continue to cook while receiving the smoke. To reduce the amount of smoke the foil package generates move it to a cooler part of the grill. To stop the production of smoke, remove the package from the coals completely. The package can easily be handled with barbecue tongs. If there are any chips remaining you can use the same package again making this method a really efficient and controllable way of producing smoke on a barbecue.

Place the foil package on hot charcoal (cold charcoal is pictured for demonstration purposes).

Cover the partially cooked food on the barbecue with an upturned metal roasting tray.

Using Roasting Trays

A simple way of improvising a hot smoker is to use two roasting trays clamped together.

1 Place a tablespoon of wood chips in the centre of the base of the first roasting dish. Place the foil tray over this and sit the rack on top.

2 Place the meat or fish directly onto the racks and secure the second roasting tray upside down over the first with bulldog clips.

3 Place the roasting tray assembly on a heat source—stovetop barbecue, or portable stove (pictured)—to gently ignite the fuel.

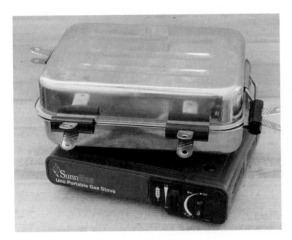

Place the roasting trays on a heat source.

INDUCTION HOB

• It is possible to use an induction stove to ignite a stovetop smoker, but the base roasting tray will need to be of a compatible material such as steel or iron and it will also need to be thick enough to maintain a rigid flat base to generate enough heat to create smoke.

• A foil smoke generator should not be used in conjunction with an induction cooling stove or induction heating source.

• Always follow the manufacturer's guidance when using this type of stove to generate heat.

ROASTING TRAY HOT SMOKER

A simple hot smoker can be easily assembled from kitchen equipment found in most homes and fuelled by a small handful of wood chips.

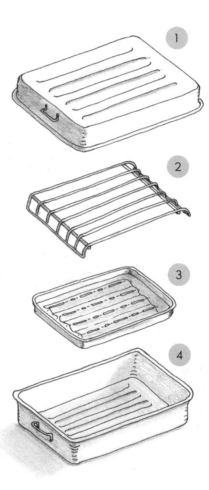

KEY

1 Upturned roasting tray
2 Food rack
3 Foil barbecue tray
4 Base roasting tray

THE SMOKING PROCESS

You have the equipment you need to either cold or hot smoke your chosen meat or fish product and now you need to consider in general terms what processes will be necessary to create your chosen dish.

Before you start to smoke any type of food product, you'll need to consider what preparatory curing may be needed. Many smoked foods should be prebrined before smoking. Brining and the use of salt in curing foods is explained on pages 18–29 and detailed instructions on the

HOT-SMOKING GUIDELINES

This table sets out broad guidelines for hot smoking a selection of meat and fish products based on a smoker temperature of 98–121°C (210–250°F). The times for smoking are given as a guide only. For best results you should use the internal temperature of the food as your main indicator that the product is cooked. Follow the instructions for smoking specific products elsewhere in the book.

PRODUCT	DRY SALTING REQUIRED	PRE-BRINING BRINE STRENGTH (SAL scale %)	SALTING/ PRE-BRINING TIME	HOT SMOKING TIME	TARGET INTERNAL TEMPERATURE
Chicken (pieces)	Yes	80%	20 minutes	25–30 minutes	74°C (165°F)
Duck (breast)	No	80%	20 minutes	15–20 minutes	74°C (165°F)
Goose (whole)	No	20%	12 hours	6–8 minutes	74°C (165°F)
Rabbit (whole)	No	40%	6 hours	45–60 minutes	74°C (165°F)
Pork spare ribs	No	No	N/A	45–60 minutes	84°C (185°F)
Turkey (whole)	No	20%	12 hours	2–4 hours	74°C (165°F)
Venison (steak)	No	40%	6 hours	20–25 minutes	74°C (165°F)
Haddock (steak)	Yes	No	N/A	20–25 minutes	72°C (160°F)
Salmon (steak)	No	80%	1 hour	20–25 minutes	68°C (155°F)
Salmon (side)	No	80%	1 hour	30–40 minutes	68°C (155°F)
Trout (whole)	No	80%	15 minutes	20–25 minutes	70°C (158°F)

process needed for specific products are given throughout this book, but the tables below provide general guidance on prebrining times and the strength of brine required.

Smoking Times

I'm often asked how long to allow food to smoke. There is no precise answer to this as the flavour of smoke on food, like that of any other seasoning, is an issue of personal taste. I prefer smoked salmon with a delicate flavour, but I know others who prefer their salmon to be more heavily smoked—sometimes for up to 36 hours. Some foods are particularly suited to heavy smoking, including beef, pork, and other strongly flavoured meats. Where you want to add flavour while retaining some of the characteristic taste of the meat or fish, it's probably best to use smoke sparingly. As mentioned earlier in the book, smoking on its own should not be relied on as the principal means of preservation, and therefore smoking times can safely be reduced when a lighter smoked flavour is required.

COLD-SMOKING GUIDELINES

The following table sets out broad guidelines for cold smoking a selection of meat and fish products. Follow the instructions for smoking specific products elsewhere in the book.

PRODUCT	PRE-BRINING TIME (Brine strength)	RINSE AND DRY	PRE-COOK	COLD SMOKING (Hours)		
				Light	Medium	Heavy
Beef fillet or lean steak	2–3 hours (80%)	Yes	No	8	24	36
Pork	1–2 hours (80%)	Yes	No	4	8	18
Lamb	2–3 hours (80%)	Yes	No	4	12	24
Chicken	2–3 hours (80%)	Yes	No	12	24	36
Duck	2–3 hours (80%)	Yes	No	12	24	36
Fish (whole)	30–60 minutes (80%)	Yes	No	4	12	24
Fish (fillet)	15–20 minutes (80%)	Yes	No	4	8	16
Prawns (raw, shell off)	15 minutes (80%)	No	Boil 10 minutes	1	2	4
Lobster (pre-boiled and shelled)	5 minutes (40%)	No	No	1	2	4

CHOOSING YOUR WOOD

Different woods add different flavour qualities to your smoked food and the way wood is prepared for smoking will influence the way it burns. Use the chart on the facing page to help you to pick the wood that best suits your smoking project. The chart on page 156 will help you select the right type of wood product for your needs.

The choice of wood type for your smoking projects is one of the most personally led aspects of the craft. Much depends on individual preference, and you can look forward to creating unusual and delicious effects by exposing your food to the smoke created from different woods.

KEY

1 Hickory	6 Beech
2 Sweet chestnut	7 Blended fuel bisquettes
3 Whisky oak	8 Apple
4 Alder	9 Oak
5 Mesquite	

TYPES OF WOOD

This chart summarizes the flavour and smoke qualities of different woods.

WOOD TYPE	AROMA NOTES	SMOKE QUALITY	GOES WELL WITH
Alder	Sweetness	Light	Pork, poultry, game, or fish
Almond	Sweetness	Heavy	Beef, lamb, pork, poultry, or game
Apple	Sweetness	Medium	Pork, poultry, or game
Apricot	Sweetness	Medium	Beef, lamb, pork, poultry, or game
Ash	Aromatic	Light	Beef, venison, game, or fish
Beech	Sweetness	Light	Pork, poultry
Birch	Sweetness	Light	Pork, poultry
Cherry	Sweetness	Medium	All meats and fish
Chestnut (sweet)	Aromatic	Light	All meats and fish
Gorse	Aromatic	Medium	All meats and fish
Grape vines	Earthy	Light	Beef, lamb, pork, poultry, or game
Hawthorn	Aromatic	Heavy	Beef. lamb, venison, or game
Hazel	Aromatic	Light	Pork, poultry, or fish
Hickory	Strong/robust	Heavy	Lamb, pork, venison, or game
Lavender	Aromatic	Light	Poultry, fish, or shellfish
Lemon	Aromatic	Medium	Beef and pork
Lilac	Aromatic	Light	Lamb, fish, or shellfish
Maple	Sweetness	Medium	Pork, poultry, or game
Mesquite	Strong/robust	Heavy	Beef, lamb, venison, or game
Mulberry	Sweetness	Light	Beef, pork, poultry, or game
Nectarine	Sweetness	Medium	All meats and fish
Oak	Strong/robust	Heavy	All meats (except poultry) and fish
Olive	Earthy	Medium	Lamb, poultry, or game
Orange	Sweetness	Medium	Beef, pork, or poultry
Peach	Earthy	Medium	Beef, lamb, pork, poultry, or game
Pear	Sweetness	Medium	Pork, poultry, game, or fish
Pecan	Aromatic	Medium	Beef, lamb, pork, poultry, or game
Plum	Sweetness	Medium	Beef, lamb, pork, poultry, or game
Rosemary	Aromatic	Light	Lamb, pork, poultry, or fish
Walnut	Strong/robust	Heavy	Beef or game
Whisky oak	Strong/robust	Heavy	Beef, pork, poultry, or fish

SELECTING A WOOD PRODUCT

Small pieces of wood are easier to light and have a natural tendency to smoulder over a long period, which can be useful when you want to cold smoke. Wood that is chipped has less tendency to smoulder and needs assistance in the form of heat or a draught to keep it smouldering. Wood from different tree species burns at different rates. Oak, for instance, is typically a slow burner, while apple or beech burn faster. Other factors also influence the way wood burns, chiefly moisture and humidity.

Refer to the following table for detail on the different burning characteristics for various preparations of smoking woods.

CHOOSING WOOD TYPES FOR BURN CHARACTERISTICS

Use this chart to help you choose the wood product that suits your food and equipment.

WOOD SIZE	BURNING CHARACTERISTICS
Fine wood dust (less than 1 mm particle size)	Smoulders slowly when the conditions are right. Likely to be affected by moisture. Unlikely to burn with a flame unless an airflow is present.
Coarse wood dust (1–2 mm particle size)	Less likely to smoulder without airflow present and likely to be affected by moisture. Unlikely to flame when burning. Dry material has a tendency to self-extinguish.
Fine chips (3–5 mm/$^1/_8$–¼ in particle size)	Tendency to smoulder if a draught is present. Affected by moisture and can flare up if a draught increases. May self-extinguish.
Coarse chips (5–13 mm/¼–½ in particle size)	Tendency to self-extinguish where there is no draught. May flame if lit when dry. May be slow to light when damp but once alight will burn. May smoulder if airflow is present.
Small chunks (13–25 mm/½–1 in)	Likely to burn on lighting when dry. May be slow to light when damp. May not smoulder without an airflow. Burns freely if stacked with sufficient ventilation.
Large chunks (25–100 mm/1–4 in)	Slow to ignite but once alight burn freely. Will smoulder if there is sufficient draught.
Disks or logs (over 100 mm/4 in)	May be slow to ignite but once alight can smoulder providing there is a draught. Logs and wood this size can burn freely if stacked with sufficient ventilation.
Shavings (5–13 mm/¼–½ in)	Tendency to ignite and can cause flare-ups, especially if there is a draught. Will smoulder if the draught is controlled and if moistened with water. May self-extinguish if too moist.

STORING SMOKED FOOD

Once you have created your smoked food, it's likely that you'll consume it quite quickly. Any leftovers will be too delicious to discard and should be stored to eat later.

Because smoke has antibacterial and antimicrobial properties, you might assume that the food will last for a little longer. This is true to some extent, but for safety you should store smoked foods in the same way as fresh foods.

Food Smells

Food that has been smoked has a characteristic smoky aroma that may affect other foods stored in the same place. In particular, storing food that has a strong aroma in the refrigerator is likely to make more delicately flavoured foods take on some of the smells and tastes. To minimize the likelihood of smells transferring onto other food in the refrigerator, store smoked food in resealable bags or containers. Enclosing your food in clingfilm won't always stop strong smells from getting out into the refrigerator.

Vacuum Packaging

One great way to make your food last longer is to vacuum pack it. Vacuum packing machines are readily available in shops and online. These machines are for domestic use only, are very easy to operate, and provide a good seal. Food that is vacuum packed lasts a lot longer than food sealed in the usual way, but this process doesn't mean you don't have to refrigerate it. This is especially true for salmon, which can carry listeria bacteria.

Refrigeration and Freezing

Keeping food cool is the key to maintaining freshness. The ideal temperature for storing cold smoked fish in a refrigerator is between 3–5°C (37–41°F). You should be able to store well-wrapped smoked salmon at this temperature for up to five days. It's worth remembering that a refrigerator with an integral ice box in the main compartment is a very dry environment, so if you don't cover up the food inside, it will have a tendency to become over dry. The coldest part of the refrigerator is at the bottom unless you have an appliance with an internal fan, in which case the temperature should be uniform throughout.

The ideal freezer temperature for long-term food storage is -18 to -23°C (0 to 10°F). Refer to the food storage instructions for your appliance for precise guidance on safe storage times.

Freezing is one of the best ways to store smoked meat and fish for extended periods.

SCOTTISH STYLE COLD-SMOKED SALMON

There is nothing finer than properly prepared, cured and cold-smoked salmon, a delicacy often reserved for special occasions. If you have only ever eaten this product from a supermarket then you are in for a treat.

KEY STAGES

1 Preparing

2 Salting

3 Drying

4 Smoking

Fresh-caught salmon is the king of fish, and cold smoking is a perfect way of preparing it.

Once you've made your own cold-smoked salmon, there is no going back to commercially smoked products, and rightly so. I still get a buzz when I walk from the smoker, cold-smoked salmon in hand, to the kitchen to rest the salmon and slice it. You'll also be surprised at the number of friends' parties and get-togethers you get invited to when they learn you can smoke salmon to order. This style of salmon – in contrast to hot-smoked salmon (page 172) – it retains much of its original flavour, oils, and texture.

Food Hygiene Considerations

Cold-smoked salmon is essentially a raw product that needs to be treated with respect in terms of food safety and hygiene. Using fresh ingredients is vitally important and if there is any doubt about the quality of the fish, don't use it.

Be sure to follow the safety and hygiene advice given on page 30. In particular, keep raw and cured fish separately, and always wash your hands between handling raw and cured products.

Initial Preparation

If you are working from a whole fish, you'll need to fillet it first. You'll find out how to do this on page 56. The second step in making cold-smoked salmon

Cold-smoked salmon is classically thinly sliced in a "D" shape (right).

is applying salt to the flesh to remove moisture and assist in preserving the fish. Cold-smoked salmon is traditionally dry salted. The application of salt allows the fish to lose a proportion of its moisture (see also pages 18–29). This is an important step as losing moisture makes it harder for bacteria to grow and also improves the texture and oil ratios in the flesh. Other ingredients such as herbs and sugars can be added to the cure at this stage, if desired (see page 25).

Drying – A Key Stage

Drying removes yet more moisture from the fish, improving the texture still further and also making it even more difficult for bacteria to grow. The time it takes to dry in the refrigerator also allows the salt levels to equalize throughout the fish and for the surface to develop a thin, sticky salt-glaze layer – the pellicle. It's important not to cover the fish in

the refrigerator during this time or it won't dry. It's worth noting that if you keep salad or other vegetables in the open part of the refrigerator, drying may take longer, as all these products release moisture.

The Smoking Process

Cold smoking salmon can take anything from 6 to 36 hours depending on your taste preference. I prefer a shorter smoking time as this preserves the flavour of the salmon and works in balance with the flavour of the fish. The temperature for cold smoking should always be below 30°C (86°F) and ideally much lower, especially if you intend to cold smoke for an extended period of time (more than eight hours). Cold smoking also continues the

Homemade cold-smoked salmon served with lemon and dill is an ideal starter.

process of drying and weight loss. In total, the overall weight loss from the raw product to the finished product could be anywhere from 10 to 20 per cent depending on the time allowed for curing, drying, and smoking. Local weather conditions and humidity play a part in this too; in moist environments weight loss is less than in a drier environment.

Slicing

Traditionally cold-smoked salmon is sliced in a style called D slicing. Working from the tail end and slicing across the width of the fillet, cuts are made on an angle slanting towards the tail. The slices should be thin enough to see the knife through the slice.

Storage

The final but no less important part of the process is storage. Temperature is critical, and if your refrigerator does not maintain a sufficiently low temperature (3°C/37°F), your smoked salmon will last a shorter time. Vacuum packaging and freezing can greatly extend the storage life of the product (see page 87).

Preparation

Fillet and pin bone the salmon as described on page 56. Trim the edges of the fillets to remove any visible fat but leave the skin in place.

Salting

1 Apply a thin layer of salt evenly over the entire surface of the fillet starting at the thickest part (the head end).

2 Apply another layer of salt to the fish. Apply more salt to the thickest part at the head end so it can cure properly. Apply only a thin layer to the tail end and the thinner edges; too much salt will over cure these parts.

Fillet and trim the salmon.

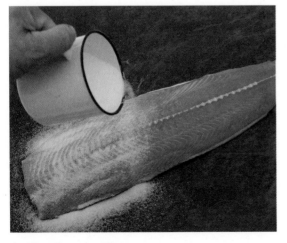

Apply salt to the fillet.

Use more salt on the thicker parts than at the tail end and edges.

Curing and Drying

1 Place the salmon in a nonreactive dish in the refrigerator for about six hours. After this time, remove it from the refrigerator and rinse under cold running water. Lay the fish on kitchen paper and pat the surface dry with more kitchen paper.

2 Return the salmon to the refrigerator. Leave the fish uncovered to dry for a minimum of 24 hours. This is an important part of the process as this is when the pellicle is formed. This is a thin, slightly sticky film that forms on the surface of the salmon, which helps the smoke stick to the fish during smoking.

Cold Smoking

1 Place the salmon skin-side down on racks in the cold smoker at a temperature below 30°C (86°F) for at least four hours.

2 Remove the fish from the smoker and allow it to rest in a cool place for 30 minutes to stabilize. The salmon can now be wrapped and refrigerated at 3°C (37°F). In these conditions it will keep for up to seven days.

Place the salmon in the smoker.

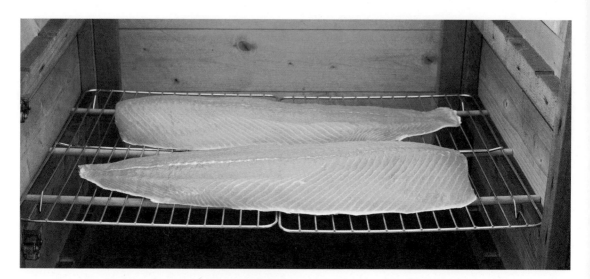

Cold-Smoked Salmon Blinis

A classic canapé, cold-smoked salmon blinis are the ideal snack for a smart drinks celebration. Bite-sized blinis – tiny Russian buckwheat pancakes – topped with cream cheese or sour cream provide an ideal base for this delicious party favourite, but you can use triangles of buttered wholegrain bread instead.

METHOD
You can buy ready-made blinis in many supermarkets. Simply place a small amount of sour cream onto each pancake. Arrange a sliver of thinly sliced smoked salmon on top. Squeeze some lemon juice over the salmon and grind some black pepper on top. Garnish with chives and crushed black pepper, or, for an added touch of luxury, spoon a small amount of lumpfish roe to complete this delicious mouthful.

COLD-SMOKED KIPPERS

Kippers are traditionally cured, cold-smoked herrings. Packed with healthy omega oils, this is a smoked fish product to relish. There is also a hot-smoked variation (see facing page), which makes a interesting change.

KEY STAGES

1 Pre-brining

2 Drying

3 Cold smoking

Kippers are traditionally eaten on their own with bread or toast.

Herrings, from which kippers are made, are a plentiful North Atlantic fish. And for hundreds of years a proportion of the large catches landed have been cured and smoked to produce kippers. Herrings that are to be used for kippers are traditionally back cut which is a process that flattens them out to give them their characteristic look. See page 48 for instructions on how to do this.

Cold Smoking

The process of producing this type of kipper starts with pre-brining. This is described on page 50. When the brined herrings are dry, they can be loaded into the smoker on racks. A low temperature is maintained to impart flavour while not cooking the fish. The temperature is then raised slightly to finish off the cold-smoking process. This helps liberate the oils from the fish giving them a lovely glaze. Be sure to read the general information on smoking earlier in this chapter (pages 132–157).

WOOD CHOICE

Herring is an oily fish and has a robust flavour. I like to smoke my kippers with oak chips because this smoke is similarly robust and gives a lovely rich colour to the finished product.

Serving and Storing

Cold-smoked kippers require cooking before they can be eaten; simply poach them for a few minutes in a shallow pan of water with a knob of butter, serve them with some crusty buttered bread and you have the perfect start to the day. You can also use the cooked fish to make a paste for a flavoursome spread on toast. Substitute kippers for bloaters in the recipe for bloater paste on page 167.

You can keep cooked kippers in the refrigerator for seven days or, providing you wrap them tightly to exclude all the air, in the freezer for three months.

Cold Smoking Kippers

1 Back cut the herrings as described on page 48 and brine them as described on page 50. Rinse and dry them.

2 Hang the herrings on pairs of hooks that have been attached to a length of wood (known as a "spate"). This method is designed to keep the kippers flat during smoking and also keep them apart while they receive the smoke.

3 Cold smoke the kippers for a minimum of eight hours. This time can be extended if you like a stronger flavour. Maintain a temperature in the cold smoker below 30°C (86°F) for the first six hours. For the last two hours, raise the temperature just above this level. If you are smoking for a longer period of time, maintain this temperature until the end of your chosen smoking time.

HOT-SMOKED VARIATION

You can, if you prefer, hot smoke your kippers. A hot-smoked kipper can be eaten straight from the smoker – it needs no further cooking and is served in the same way as a cold-smoked kipper.

• Prepare in the same way as for cold smoking up to the smoking stage. Then lay the fish on individual wire racks in the hot smoker so that they are not touching one another. Bring the temperature of the smoker up to 30°C (86°F) and smoke the herrings for one hour.

• After one hour raise the temperature in the smoker to 85°C (185°F) and smoke the kipper until the internal temperature of the fish has reached 75°C (167°F). You can check this with a meat thermometer. Remove the kipper from the smoker and allow the fish to rest and cool.

Hook the kippers onto a length of wood.

Hang the kippers in the cold smoker.

BLOATERS

Not to be confused with the fish of the same name native to the Great Lakes of North America, bloaters are cured and cold-smoked whole herrings. If you like the strong smoky flavour of kippers, you'll love bloaters, which can be best describe as a gamey version of kippers.

KEY STAGES

1 Dry salting

2 Smoking

Bloaters are prepared from fresh herring with their heads on and the guts in. After dry salting, they are traditionally cold-smoked over either oak or beech. The finished product has a subtle and delicate flavour that is less salty than most kippers.

Storage
Bloaters can be stored in the refrigerator for up to a week at around 3°C (37°F) but ideally they should be eaten within three days. Bloaters can also be frozen for up to three months providing they are well wrapped in sturdy plastic bags.

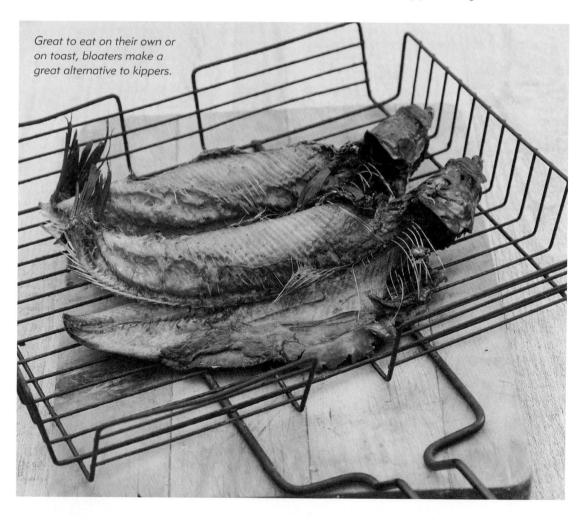

Great to eat on their own or on toast, bloaters make a great alternative to kippers.

Making Bloaters

1 Lay the herrings in a nonreactive dish on a 1-cm (½-in) layer of salt. Then completely cover the fish with salt. If the dish is deep enough, you can lay the herring on top of each other separated by a thin layer of salt. Refrigerate and allow to cure for a day before rinsing the salt off and drying.

2 Spear the salted herrings through the head with a thin rod of wood. Hang the fish in a cold smoker and smoke for about 12 hours. Because the cold-smoking process is not hot enough to cook the fish, bloaters need further cooking before they can be eaten (see Cooking and Serving Bloaters, below).

Spear the herrings on a wooden rod.

Suspend the fish in a cold smoker.

Cooking and Serving Bloaters

Bloaters can be grilled or baked or, if you prefer, cooked on a barbecue.
For all methods, lightly score both sides of the fish and smear in melted butter.

Grilling To grill them, add a squeeze of lemon to both sides and cook until the skin begins to crisp up. Turn and repeat on the other side.

Baking To bake a bloater, place on a sheet of baking parchment and add a couple of slices of lemon to the package and seal it closed. Bake for 20 minutes in a preheated oven at 150°C (300°F).

Barbecuing To barbecue your bloaters, cook for three minutes directly above hot coals on both sides. Remove to a cooler part of the barbecue and cover with foil for a further five minutes.

Making Bloater Paste To make a paste to spread on toast, simply take the flesh from two baked bloaters. Remove all the bones and add an equal weight of softened butter. Add the juice of one lemon and one teaspoon each of ground black pepper and cayenne pepper. Blend all the ingredients together until you have a smooth paste. Place in ramekins and cover with melted butter infused with a few strands of saffron.

COLD-SMOKED BACON

The distinctive aroma of your first batch of home-cured smoked bacon sizzling in the pan – and it's mouth-watering flavour – will almost certainly mean you'll never want to go back to supermarket bacon ever again.

KEY STAGES

1 Curing

2 Resting

3 Smoking

The technique described on these pages is for a sweet-cured bacon. Bacon benefits particularly from the combination of sweetness and smoke. Sugars and other forms of natural sweetness take away some of the harsh saltiness that can accompany heavily cured bacon. Sweet-cured and cold-smoked bacon follows the same initial curing process as dry-cured bacon (see page 66), the difference consisting of the addition of sugar to the cure mix. For this type of sweet-cured bacon, sugar makes up about a quarter of the whole cure mix. Remember that cold-smoking produces a product that requires further cooking before consumption. The basics of cold smoking are set out on pages 132–147.

Aroma and Flavour

Cold-smoking is a gentle process that imparts a lovely wood smoke flavour and aroma to the bacon, and as bacon is a robust meat with it's own distinctive salty taste, the flavour of the smoke you use with it should be able to stand up to this competition, complementing the other elements where possible. Bacon is traditionally smoked with oak, beech, or hickory. Of these three smokes, beech is the mildest with oak and hickory producing heavier smoke with plenty of flavour. Even at the relatively cool temperatures used for cold-smoking (under 30°C/86°F), as the bacon smokes

Cold-smoked bacon can be made from several different cuts of pork, including loin, back, and belly pork.

it continues to dry, improving its texture and flavour. The time needed for cold smoking bacon is largely a matter of personal taste, but if you want a really robust flavour, smoke it for 8 to 12 hours using oak or hickory. If you want a lighter flavour, try beech for four hours. Oak smoke offers an added bonus of producing a lovely colour, as well as being full of flavour.

Smoking Setup

You can suspend the bacon either on hooks high inside the smoker or you can place it on a wire rack. The results will essentially be the same. I prefer laying the bacon down as the smoke tends to settle on the upper surface of the meat, which adds more flavour. But depending on the configuration and space in your smoker, your choice may be different. Both methods produce sound results.

Resting Time

When you've finished smoking the bacon, remove it from the smoker and wrap it loosely in greaseproof paper. Place it in a cool place such as a refrigerator to rest for 24 hours. This will allow some of the lighter smoke residue to disperse leaving the more enduring flavours and aromas behind. Anyone who has eaten smoked food on the same day will tell you that the flavours can be a little strong.

ALTERNATIVE SOURCES OF SWEETNESS

Added sweetness for bacon doesn't have to come from sugar. You can use honey, maple syrup, or even liquorice. Maple syrup and honey can be substituted weight for weight with sugar to achieve the same results. If you choose to use liquorice instead of sugar, use pure fine liquorice powder – about one teaspoonful for each kilogram (2¼ lb) of bacon.

Cold Smoking Bacon

1 Dry cure the pork as described on page 66. When the curing is complete, wash and dry the meat and place it in the refrigerator for a day. This "resting time" will help to form a pellicle – the thin sticky film formed by the salt from the cure and the natural fluids on the surface of the bacon. The pellicle will help the smoke stick to the bacon when it goes in the smoker.

2 Hang the bacon in the cold smoker from stainless steel hooks. Insert two hooks through the skin of the bacon in each corner of the meat and suspend it high in the smoker. Alternatively, you can place the bacon on a wire rack skin side down. Make sure all sides of the bacon will be exposed to smoke and are not touching the sides of the smoker.

3 Cold smoke the meat to the strength you prefer, which could take from 4 (light flavour) to 24 hours (strong flavour). When the cold smoking is complete, loosely wrap the bacon in greaseproof paper and place it in the refrigerator for 24 hours to mellow before slicing. Refrigeration will also make the bacon firmer and therefore easier to slice.

YOU WILL NEED

- **1 kg (2¼ lb) piece of pork (loin, back, or belly pork)**

FOR THE CURE

- **2 tbs. salt**
- **2 tsp. soft brown sugar**
- **½ tsp. Prague Powder #1**

Rinse and dry the meat after dry curing.

Hang the meat in the cold smoker.

HOT-SMOKED BACON

After dry-salting, you can choose to hot smoke your bacon. The timing for hot smoking bacon depends on the size of the piece of meat. Hot smoking is complete when the internal temperature of the meat reaches 72°C (160°F). When hot smoking bacon, the temperature in the smoker normally has to reach or exceed at least 94°C (200°F). During hot-smoking the bacon will release fat and juices, from the meat so it's a good idea to place a tray under the wire rack to catch any drips. During the smoking process, you can baste the bacon surface with maple syrup for a sweet finish.

After smoking allow the meat to cool to room temperature before refrigerating it. The finished product can be sliced thinly like ham and eaten without further preparation, or it can be fried.

Best Bacon Sandwich

Home-cured bacon combines beautifully with lettuce, tomato, and mayonnaise along with fresh-baked bread to make one of the best sandwiches for a sustaining brunch or snack while watching the match. Simple to make, the freshness and flavours of the ingredients make this a favourite with all the family.

INGREDIENTS

For one sandwich you will need:
- 4 slices of cold-smoked bacon
- 2 slices of fresh bread
- 3–4 leaves of crisp lettuce
- 1 large tomato (thinly sliced)
- 1 tbsp. mayonnaise
- 2 tsp. soft butter
- Salt and black pepper to taste

METHOD

1 Fry the bacon until crisp. Set aside on sheets of kitchen paper. Drain excess fat from the pan and rub both slices of the bread in the pan to lightly coat the inside faces of the bread with the bacon fat.

2 Remove the bread from the pan and lightly spread with butter. Lay the lettuce leaves and slices of tomato on one of the slices of bread, followed by the bacon. Season with salt and black pepper and spread the mayonnaise on the other slice of bread. Close the sandwich and serve.

HOT-SMOKED SALMON

This method of preparation lends a delicate yet distinctive flavour to this succulent fish. Hot smoking a salmon can easily be undertaken either outside in a hot-smoker or inside on a domestic kitchen stove.

Salmon is a robust fish with a distinctive flavour and firm texture, but like any fish, it is quite easy to overcook it, leading to an over-dry texture that is not ideal. Therefore temperature control is an important part of the process of hot smoking this fish. The aim is to prevent the heat exceeding 75°C (167°F). To achieve this control you will need a hot smoker with a built-in temperature gauge or have a hand-held meat thermometer that you can insert into the thickest part of the salmon. When you've been hot-smoking meat and fish for a while, you'll instinctively get a feel for how long and how hot is going to be enough.

Before smoking, the salmon needs to be lightly brined to provide seasoning. The salt used in the brine also interacts with the flavours in the smoke to enhance the flavour of the fish still further.

Serving and Storing

You can serve hot-smoked salmon straight from the smoker if you like, but it will taste better if allowed to rest for a short while. Resting allows some of the harsher smoke compounds to dissipate. To store your hot smoked salmon, allow the salmon to cool completely and then refrigerate for one hour or until the salmon is completely cool. Wrap the salmon tightly in clingfilm or place in a vacuum bag and seal. The salmon will keep in the refrigerator for up to five days or it will freeze well for up to six months.

Served with vegetables or beans and a garnish of fresh salad leaves, hot-smoked salmon can be the centrepiece of a highly nutritious meal.

Preparation and Brining

1 Either buy ready cut salmon steaks of prepare your own from a whole salmon. In the latter case, follow the instructions on filleting a whole salmon (page 56) to the point where you have a side that has been pin-boned and with the rib bones removed, but the skin is still in place. The reason for leaving the skin in place is to provide some stability to the fish. Now cut the fish into steaks approximately 50 mm (2 in) wide.

2 Prepare a brine solution and brine the salmon as described on pages 62–63.

3 When the brining is completed, remove the salmon from the brine and pat dry. There is no need to rinse. Allow the salmon to rest in the refrigerator for about two hours before smoking. This will allow the fish to dry a little.

Submerge the salmon steaks in brine.

ADDED FLAVOUR

It's possible to add some additional flavours to the brine for hot-smoked salmon (see page 26). Try adding some fresh grated ginger for great flavour and aroma. If you are going to turn your finished smoked salmon into pâté, it's probably best to avoid adding flavours during brining as the recipe may contain additional flavours that could clash.

Smoking

1 Pre-set your hot smoker to 85°C (185°F) and allow it to come up to temperature.

2 Place the salmon on an open rack in the smoker and smoke until the internal temperature of the fish reaches 75°C (167°F). Turn off the heat and continue to smoke for a further 15 minutes. Remove the salmon from the smoker and allow to rest until completely cool. The salmon is now ready to eat.

TOP LIP TEST

If you're not sure of the temperature of the fish and you don't have a meat thermometer, insert a metal skewer into the thickest part of the fish for a couple of seconds. Remove it and carefully touch it on your skin just above your top lip. If it feels hot then the fish is done. This is an old chef's method.

Pre-heat the hot smoker.

Check the temperature of the fish.

Hot-Smoked Salmon Niçoise

A classic salad usually made with tuna, that when made with hot-smoked salmon, provides an original and flavoursome summer lunchtime treat.

INGREDIENTS

- **2 hot-smoked salmon steaks (skin removed)**
- **4 medium ripe cherry tomatoes (halved)**
- **2 hardboiled eggs (cooled, shelled, and quartered)**
- **100 g (4 oz) salad leaves**
- **50-mm (2-in) piece of cucumber**
- **220 g (8 oz) new potatoes**
- **50 g (2 oz) green beans**
- **50 g (2 oz) anchovy fillets**
- **50 g (2 oz) black olives (pitted)**
- **4 spring onions**

Serves 2

METHOD

1 Cut the green beans into 2-in. (50-mm) pieces and blanch. Slice the spring onions finely, and dice the cucumber.

2 Just before serving, arrange the salad leaves, tomatoes, cucumber, new potatoes, beans, and spring onions in a large salad bowl. Place chunks of hot-smoked salmon and egg quarters on top of the salad, followed by the anchovy fillets and black olives.

3 Dress the salad with a simple vinaigrette. Serve with warm, crusty bread.

HOT-SMOKED TROUT

Hot-smoking works brilliantly with trout, and is really easy to do at home. Hot-smoked trout is delicious on it's own and is a foundation ingredient in many tasty recipes.

Good-quality farmed trout are easy to obtain. Most shop-bought trout weigh about 220 g (8 oz) and this is a perfect size for hot-smoking. The trout should first be gutted and the skin washed. You can do this yourself, following the instructions for gutting mackerel on page 53. But if you prefer, a helpful fishmonger will usually do this for you. The process includes a stage of pre-brining, which adds flavour to the fish and also enhances the smoke flavour.

Smoking Set-up

I use a large stovetop smoker to hot-smoke trout, but if you haven't got one, you can improvise by sandwiching together two identical roasting tins using bulldog clips. This is the method I have described here (see also page 151).

KEY STAGES
1 Pre-brining
2 Drying
3 Smoking

YOU WILL NEED
• **2 trout (about 8 oz/225 g in weight)**
• **Salt**
• **2 lemons**
• **Bunch of fresh parsley**

Preparing and Pre-brining the Trout

1 Gut and clean the trout as described on page 53. I prefer to keep the heads on the fish when hot smoking trout, but, if you prefer to remove them, shorten the cooking time a little.

2 Make up a batch of 80 per cent (SAL scale) brine as described on page 28, ensuring it is refrigerated before use. You'll need enough brine to cover the fish. Place the gutted trout in a nonreactive dish, pour over the brine to cover the fish, and place in the refrigerator for 15 minutes.

3 Remove the fish from the brine and rinse under cold running water and pat dry with kitchen paper.

The cavity of the trout can be stuffed with lemon and fresh herbs to impart a delicate flavour to the flesh (left).

Hot-smoked trout make a simple, but rewarding smoking project (right).

Preparing the Smoker

1 Place one heaped tablespoon of wood chips or dust into the bottom of the smoker or roasting dish roughly in the centre, directly above the heat source. Cover the wood with a sheet of aluminium foil. Alternatively, you can use a foil barbecue tray with holes in. Place an oiled roasting rack or roasting trivet on top of the foil to support the trout above the smoldering wood, allowing the smoke to circulate freely.

2 Place the trout onto the roasting rack. Cut a couple of slices of lemon and some parsley and place these into the gut cavity of each fish. This adds some lovely flavours while holding open the gut cavity to allow the smoke in.

3 Fix the second roasting tin upside down over the first, securing the two together with binder clips (see also page 151).

Smoking

1 Place the improvised hot smoker on the stove. If you have a good extractor fan, you can do this on your kitchen stove over a medium heat (not too high) for 20 minutes. Alternatively, use a portable stove outside, in which case it may need to smoke for an additional five minutes. When the smoking time is up, remove the smoker from the heat, and allow it to stand for five minutes. This will let any remaining smoke to dissipate and let the trout cook through.

2 Remove the lid and use a fish slice to place the trout on a plate. Test the fish in its thickest part with skewer or thermometer to ensure it is cooked through. The trout is now ready to eat or can be used to make a wonderful trout pâté (see facing page).

Place wood chips in the centre of a roasting tray smoker.

Stuff the fish with lemon and parsley.

Set the smoker on the heat source.

SKINNING TIP

Hot trout is much easier to skin, so if you are considering turning your smoked trout into pâté, it's worth taking the fish apart while it's still warm.

Hot-Smoked Trout Pâté

This is a simple recipe for a delicious starter that works equally well for smoked mackerel.

INGREDIENTS

- 2 whole hot-smoked trout (225 g/ 8 oz each)
- 50 g (2 oz) unsalted butter (softened)
- Juice of 1 lemon
- 2 tbsp. creamed horseradish
- Large pinch of cayenne pepper
- Large pinch of freshly grated nutmeg
- Freshly ground black pepper
- 105 ml (7 tbsp.) sour cream or crème fraîche
- 4 tbsp. chopped chives

TO SERVE

- Mixed salad leaves
- 2 lemons, cut into wedges
- Plenty of slices of freshly toasted bread

Serves 8

METHOD

1 Remove the skin from the fish and, using a fork, remove the fillets from the bone. Ensure you remove all the bones and skin from the fish. Place the roughly flaked the fillets into the bowl of a food processor.

2 Add the softened butter, half the lemon juice, horseradish, cayenne pepper, and nutmeg, and season well with black pepper. Pulse to combine. You can also combine the ingredients by hand using a fork.

3 Transfer the mixture to a bowl and fold in the sour cream. Add the chives and stir well to combine. Check the seasoning, adding more lemon juice if required.

Serve in individual ramekin dishes with a handful of salad leaves, wedges of lemon, and slices of toast.

HOT-SMOKED HADDOCK

Haddock is a white fish that combines well with smoke. Hot-smoked, it is a key ingredient in many dishes including fish pies and chowders, but it also has the character to stand up as a dish on its own.

KEY STAGES
1 Salting
2 Drying
3 Smoking

Haddock is a North Atlantic cold-water fish. Haddock is meaty with lovely large flakes and a distinctive flavour. Over the years haddock has been viewed as inferior to cod, which has held first place in the white fish popularity stakes – unjustly in my opinion. The flavour of haddock goes wonderfully well with a smoky aroma.

Traditional Delight

The Arbroath Smokie is perhaps the most famous example of a hot-smoked haddock delicacy. It is prepared from the whole fish, minus the head, dry-salted for a short time, and rinsed in cold, fresh water. Tied in pairs by the tail, the fish are laid across wooden spates (frames) to drain and dry, and then hot-smoked over oak or beech. In the past these fires were set into half barrels that were lined with slate or flat stones to protect them. The fish were covered over with sacking to keep the heat and moisture in and the sack was wetted with water.

Haddock Steaks the Arbroath Way

If you have the time, inclination, and, of course, the whole fish, preparing haddock the Arbroath way is worth a try. But whole haddock are not always easy to get hold of unless you live near the sea or have access to an excellent fishmonger. Fillets are much more readily available for most people and can be bought from most supermarkets.

Hot-smoking a haddock steak is relatively straightforward. Like most white fish, haddock doesn't need heavy salting. The flesh is quite light and the salt is absorbed very quickly indeed. A light dusting of salt is all that is required before hot-smoking and this should be removed by rinsing before the fish is placed in the hot-smoker.

A Two-Stage Process

Temperature control is king when smoking fish and if you're making hot-smoked haddock to add to a dish that will be cooked further, it's best to hot-smoke the fish so it's only barely cooked. This is not as difficult as it sounds, especially if you have a smoker with effective temperature control.

The technique is a two-stage smoking process in which you start at a low temperature and gradually increase it until the internal temperature of the haddock steak at its thickest point just reaches 71°C (160°F). The fish can then be removed from the smoker and allowed to cool. This technique relies on the fish being re-heated above 75°C (167°F) in whichever dish you are using it to complete the cooking. If you're aiming to eat the fish straight from the smoker then aim for an internal temperature of 75°C (167°F).

The first stage of smoking gives the fish the opportunity to take on some smoke and colour without over-cooking. This is done by setting the smoker to a temperature of around 50°C (120°F) for up to 20 minutes. In this time the fish will take

Home-smoked haddock is a delicacy quite unlike its commercial equivalent.

on a good flavour and it will darken too. The next stage is to raise the smoker temperature to 85°C (185°F). Use a meat thermometer to gauge the rise in temperature inside the fish until it reaches 75°C (167°F). The fish can then be removed from the smoker and eaten.

Salting and Drying the Haddock

1 Sprinkle a very thin layer of salt across the surface of the fish. Place the fish skin side down in a nonreactive dish and cover with clingfilm and place in the refrigerator.

2 After 20 minutes remove the fish from the refrigerator and rinse under cold running water to remove all traces of salt from the surface. Pat dry and return the fish to the refrigerator in an uncovered dish for an hour to dry.

Smoking

1 Bring the temperature of the hot-smoker up to 30°C (86°F) and smoke the haddock for 30 minutes. After 30 minutes, raise the temperature of the smoker to 85°C (185°F) and continue to smoke the haddock until the internal temperature of the fish reaches 75°C (167°F).

2 When the fish has reached this temperature, remove it from the smoker and allow it to cool. The haddock can be eaten warm straight from the smoker, but the flavours will mellow and become more rounded if the fish is allowed to rest for a while before serving.

YOU WILL NEED
- **Haddock steak or fillet (skin on)**
- **Salt**

Sprinkle a thin layer of salt on the haddock fillets.

Place the haddock fillets in the hot smoker.

TIPS

• Leave the skin on the fish when you're hot-smoking; it will help to keep the pieces whole.

• Keep the internal temperature of the fish below 75°C (167°F) to prevent it over-drying.

• Insert a meat thermometer into the thickest part of the fish to measure the internal temperature accurately.

Classic Kedgeree

If you love the flavours of India and you love fish there is no better way to marry
the two together than in a kedgeree. This dish makes a delicious
starter or light lunch, or can be served as a complete meal.

INGREDIENTS

- **680 g (1½ lb) hot-smoked haddock**
- **2 large hardboiled eggs (cooled, shelled, and quartered)**
- **2 bay leaves**
- **170 g (6 oz) long-grain rice**
- **1 tbsp. vegetable oil**
- **1 cm (½ in) piece of fresh ginger (grated)**
- **1 bunch of spring onions (chopped)**
- **1 clove of garlic (grated)**
- **2 tbsp. hot curry powder**
- **1 tbsp. black mustard seeds**
- **Juice of half a lemon**
- **2 handfuls fresh chives or coriander leaves (chopped)**
- **1 red chilli (finely chopped)**
- **200 ml (16 fl oz) of water**

Serves 4

METHOD

1 Add the fish and bay leaves to a shallow pan of water. Bring to the boil, reduce the heat, and cover. Simmer for about five minutes.

2 Remove the fish from the pan and leave to cool. Remove the skin and flake the fish.

3 Heat the oil in a pan with a knob of butter and add the ginger, spring onions, and garlic. Soften for five minutes and add the curry powder, mustard seeds, and rice. Stir to coat the rice with the spices and herbs.

4 Add the water to the rice and bring to the boil. Simmer until the rice is cooked and all the liquid has been absorbed.

5 Add the flaked haddock to the rice and mix in the chilli and the chives or coriander leaves. Add the quartered eggs and stir gently. Place in a warm dish to serve.

SWEET AND STICKY HOT-SMOKED RIBS

Hot-smoked over coals or in a smoker, pork ribs are a creation that is hard to forget. This barbecue favourite can be marinated and seasoned to suit your own taste.

Pork ribs are an inexpensive and delicious part of the pig. Any good butcher can supply a rack to satisfy your needs. Usually a rack of ribs will contain about 12 or 13 ribs, but sometimes as few as eight.

Know Your Ribs

Baby back ribs are usually smaller than spare ribs and are taken from smaller pigs. These ribs are taken from the part of the ribs that joins the loin and are not usually longer than about 10 cm (4 in). They are easy to tell apart from spare ribs as baby back ribs have a pronounced curve in them. Spare ribs, taken from the part of the rib cage that has cartilage at the end where the ribs meet at the sternum, are much flatter and larger.

Preparation

Preparing ribs for the smoker is quite simple. You'll need to remove any excess fat and sinew from the rack as well as any silvery membrane from the inside surface of the ribs. If you don't remove this membrane, it will become brittle during cooking, and a little impervious, which is likely to impede its absorption of the smoke flavour.

I recommend trimming the ribs so they are neat and square. With the ribs all prepared in this way, you're ready to apply the marinade of your choice to the surface before smoking. Whatever combination of ingredients you use, the procedure for applying the marinade is as described on the following pages.

KEY STAGES
1 Trimming
2 Applying the marinade
3 Smoking

Hot-smoked ribs are an unsurpassed party favourite.

Trimming and Marinading the Meat

1 Trim all loose fat and sinew from the ribs, then remove the thin white membrane covering the ribs from the inside surface. Working from one end of the rack, lift up an edge of the membrane with the point of a knife. Grip the edge of the membrane with your fingers and pull the whole membrane off in one movement. Sometimes the membrane is a little slippery to hold. If this is the case use kitchen paper to improve your grip.

2 Mix the ingredients for the marinade and apply to the ribs on both sides, cover in clingfilm and set aside for a minimum of 30 minutes. Meanwhile, bring the hot smoker up to a temperature of 120°C (250°F).

Trim visible fat from the meat.

Apply the marinade to the meat.

YOU WILL NEED
- **An 8-rib rack of pork ribs**

FOR THE MARINADE:
- **2 tbsp. honey**
- **1 tbsp. salt**
- **2 tbsp. light soy sauce**
- **2 tbsp. tomato ketchup**
- **1 tsp. garlic powder**

FOR BASTING:
- **2 tbsp. honey**
- **2 tbsp. light soy sauce**
- **2 tbsp. tomato ketchup**

Smoking

1 After the allotted standing time, drain any liquid from the ribs and place them on a rack in the smoker over a tray. Smoke for one hour. Baste with the basting mix periodically during smoking.

2 You will know that the ribs are done when the internal temperature exceeds 85°C (185°F). This can be difficult to judge because the meat layer of ribs is quite thin and the bones absorb heat at a different rate to the meat. One of the best ways to test is to lift the ribs at one end with a pair of tongs and check to see if the meat begins to part from the bone.

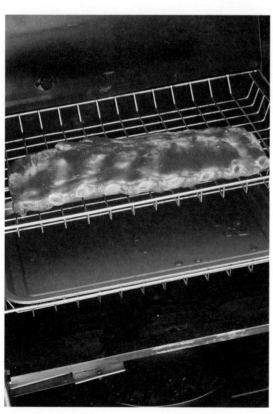

Place the meat in the hot smoker with a tray to catch the drips.

ALTERNATIVE FLAVOUR

HOT CHILLI SPARE RIBS
When using this marinade, there is no need to baste during smoking.

1 tbsp. salt
2 tbsp. paprika
2 tbsp. tomato ketchup
1 tsp. garlic powder
1 tsp. hot chilli powder

TIPS

• Always remove the thin white membrane from the inside surface of the ribs as this can stop the smoke penetrating the meat, and can also be tough to eat.

• Most marinades require a similar application. Remember that baby back ribs are a little smaller than spare ribs so they need a less time to absorb the flavours and also cook quicker.

Smoked and Sticky Spare Ribs with Spicy Barbecue Sauce

If you like your ribs hot, then try this marinade and basting sauce for a special kick.

INGREDIENTS

- An 8-rib rack of pork ribs
- 4 tbsp. tomato ketchup
- 2 tbsp. honey
- 2 tbsp. Worcestershire sauce
- 1 tsp. chilli powder
- 1 tsp. ground cumin
- 1 tsp. paprika
- 1 tsp. garlic powder
- 1 tsp. Tabasco sauce

METHOD

1 Mix the sauce ingredients and apply half the liquid to the pork ribs 1 hour before you put them in the hot smoker.

2 While the ribs are smoking, from time to time brush on more of the spicy barbecue sauce to keep the ribs moist. Just before the ribs are done, brush with the spicy barbecue sauce again and allow to finish in the smoker. Serve with chunky-cut potato wedges and extra dipping sauce for a finger-licking feast.

HOT-SMOKED CHICKEN PORTIONS

Cooked in a smoker or in the smoke of a barbecue, using hickory, oak, beech, or fruit woods, chicken pieces prepared in this way are great to eat hot or cold, on their own or as part of a more elaborate meal.

KEY STAGES

1 Seasoning

2 Smoking

Chicken is a popular and healthy alternative to red meat and it can be given a mouthwateringly original slant by the hot-smoking process. Prepared using this technique, the chicken is ready to eat straight away – a real bonus.

Preparation and Seasoning

Preparing chicken to hot smoke couldn't be easier. For this technique it's best to use chicken portions. You can buy chicken pieces ready to use, or if you have a whole chicken, you can cut it into portions yourself by following the instructions on page 46. There is no need to brine the chicken, the pieces can simply be rubbed with salt and additional flavourings to add enhance the taste and prepare the meat for the barbecue or grill. Some dry rub seasonings are described on the facing page.

Smoking Technique

Hot-smoking chicken on a barbecue grill using charcoal needs care and attention to avoid overcooking or burning the chicken. Breast cuts cook without producing much fat, but thighs, drumsticks, and wings can exude quite a lot of fat during cooking, which can lead to flare-ups on the barbecue. To prevent this, make sure you trim

Hot-smoked checken served with homemade sides makes for a perfect light lunch.

ALTERNATIVE FLAVOURS

You can create interesting flavour combinations by adding herbs and spices to the salt seasoning before smoking. These rubs can be used for both the hot smoker and the charcoal grill barbecue methods. The quantities given are sufficient for a whole chicken divided into portions. Whichever seasoning you choose, mix all the ingredients together and coat the chicken in the mixture. Massage it into the flesh and under the skin where possible. Cover and leave the meat to stand in the refrigerator for **30 minutes** before hot smoking.

1 PAPRIKA, THYME, AND GARLIC DRY RUB
1 tbsp. salt
2 tbsp. paprika
1 tsp. dried or fresh thyme leaves
1 tsp. garlic powder
½ tsp. cracked black pepper

2 TRADITIONAL HERB WET RUB
1 tbsp. salt
3 tbsp. olive oil
1 tsp. dried or fresh thyme leaves
1 tsp. dried sage
½ tsp. cracked black pepper

3 CAJUN-STYLE DRY RUB
1 tbsp. salt
1 tbsp. paprika
1 tsp. ground cumin
1 tsp. oregano
1 tsp. garlic powder
½ tsp. cracked black pepper

as much visible fat from the chicken as possible. Another tip that works if you have a barbecue with a lid is to use an offset method for cooking. This method is described on page 190. The chicken is cooked by the trapped heat and not directly by the heat from the coals. This method also helps to keep the meat moist. Temperatures in a typical charcoal barbecue can rise to 150°C (300°F) quite quickly

so you'll need to be vigilant and control the heat by adjusting the air vents. Ideally you should aim for a temperature of 110–120°C (230–250°F).

Chicken cooked in a purpose-built hot smoker is a real treat. This method is also described (see page 191). The meat cooks slowly and maintains its moistness, which is often lost during conventional roasting. And the flavour is great!

Seasoning the Chicken Portions

Lightly season the chicken portions simply with salt or apply one third of your chosen seasoning mix (see page 189).

Caramelizing the Skin

1 Light the barbecue and when the flames have subsided, place the seasoned chicken on a rack over the coals for three minutes. This caramelizes the skin, providing lots of flavour and colour.

2 Turn the chicken, sprinkle salt or apply a further third of your chosen seasoning mix on the cooked side. Cook the other side for another three minutes. Turn the chicken a second time and apply the remaining seasoning.

Smoking

1 Rake the coals to one end of the grill and place the chicken portions at the other end of the grill so that they are not directly above the coals. Add a foil packet containing your chosen wood chips to the coals and close the lid on your barbecue.

2 Allow the chicken to smoke and cook through in the heat for 30 minutes, checking the temperature within the barbecue to ensure it stays between 110–120°C (230 and 250°F).

Checking the Temperature

To check the chicken is properly cooked, insert a knife into the flesh and if the juices run clear, with no sign of redness, it's done. You can also check with a meat thermometer. If the internal temperature of the meat has reached 74°C (165°F), it is sufficiently cooked.

Lightly salt the chicken portions.

Place the chicken on a hot barbecue.

Turn the pieces and add more seasoning.

Move the chicken away from the coals.

Check the internal temperature of the chicken with a meat thermometer.

Hot-Smoker Method

1 Pre-heat your hot-smoker to a temperature of 110°C (230°F).

2 Season the chicken portions with salt or seasoning mix on both sides and place on the smoking rack. Place the rack high in the smoker and place place a metal tray beneath to catch any drips. This will help to keep the inside of your smoker clean.

3 Leave the chicken in the smoker until it is cooked (see Checking the Temperature, facing page). Remove it from the smoker and allow it to rest for a short time.

Place the seasoned chicken in the hot smoker.

HOT-SMOKED WHOLE TURKEY

Turkey is a very popular bird at any time of year. The lovely thing about this bird is that there's a lot of meat on it and when it's smoked the result is mouth-watering. Here you'll learn how to prepare succulent hot-smoked turkey.

KEY STAGES

1 Pre-brining

2 Smoking

Turkey is not only one of the best types of poultry for smoking, but it is also widely available. The main issue to consider is the size of the bird. Turkeys can be very large, they have thick parts and they have thin parts. Their physical size may make it impossible for you to fit it into your smoker, so you may need to divide it into smaller portions or pieces. The method for smoking turkey pieces is similar to that used for chicken (page 188) or goose (page 196).

Gauging the Temperature

To ensure your bird is cooked through you need to aim for an internal temperature in excess of 74°C (165°F). Taking a temperature reading in a large bird is relatively easy because you have a large area to choose from. I always check the thickest part of the breast in at least two places and I check the thighs too as these can be thick in parts.

Size Considerations

Because a turkey can be large, you'll need a refrigerator with enough space to accommodate the brining container (see page 194). In addition, the smoking times tend to be long. This poses a risk of the meat near the surface becoming excessively dry. One way around this is to place a tray of warm water in the smoker after the first two hours of smoking. The water stabilizes the temperature inside the smoker. Some smokers have a water tray fitted as standard. In an electric smoker the water acts to humidify the atmosphere as the smoking

continues at the specified temperature. The reason for using warm water is to prevent the temperature in the smoker being reduced as a result of the need to heat the water in the pan. You may need to top the water up from time to time so be sure to check the level every hour or so.

Another concern is the length of time it may take to heat the turkey, especially if the heat source is inefficient and the turkey has come straight out of the refrigerator. If after four or five hours in the smoker, the internal temperature of the bird has not reached at least 60°C (140°F), remove it from the smoker and complete the cooking in the oven. Once the temperature of the bird has reached the target internal temperature of 74°C (165°F), it can be removed from the oven and returned to the smoker to cool down while getting another dose of smoke to finish off.

Choosing a Turkey

For smoking purposes, I recommend a small bird of a maximum weight of 5 kg (11 lb). Larger turkeys will take too long to smoke in most cases.

The golden colour of a hot-smoked turkey creates an appetizing prospect.

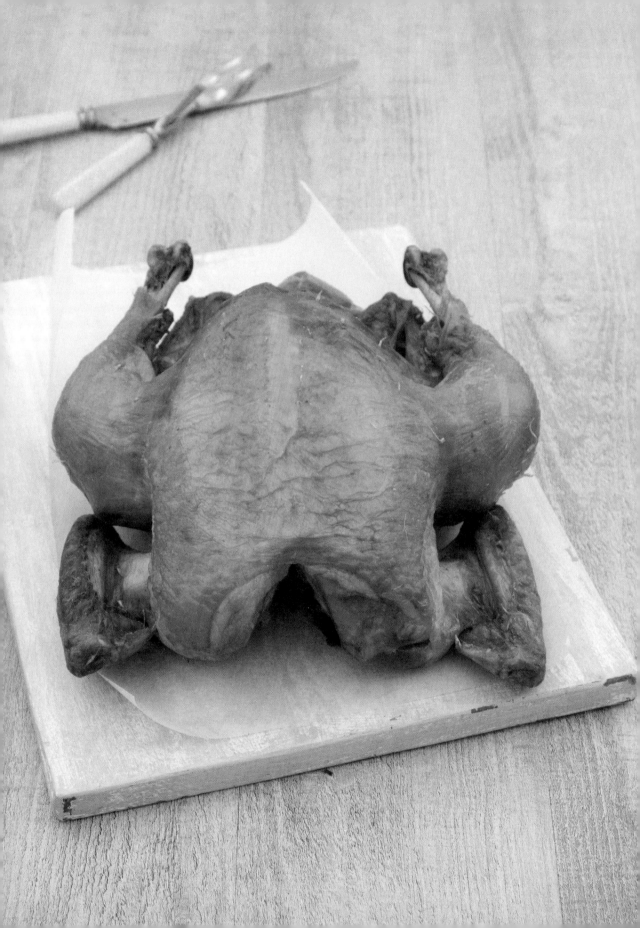

Pre-Brining

1 Mix the brine in a container made of nonreactive materials that is large enough to fit your turkey. Make a weak brine solution of 20 per cent (SAL scale) – 55 g of salt per litre of water. Into this brine solution, you can add, according to choice, sugar, honey, or some herbs and spices. Mix all the ingredients together and stir until all the salt is dissolved. Chill the brine to 4°C (39°F).

2 Immerse the turkey in the chilled brine so that the bird is completely submerged and no air is trapped in the cavity. You may need to rest a plate or some other weight on top of the bird to ensure it stays submerged. Sometimes it's easier to immerse the bird breast side down as this presents a flatter surface on which to rest a weight.

3 Brine the turkey in the refrigerator for 12 hours. Remove the bird from the tub, drain the brine from the cavity, and pat the whole bird dry with kitchen paper. Allow the turkey to rest at room temperature for an hour.

Smoking

1 Pre-heat the smoker to 110°C (230°F). Place the turkey on a wire rack. If possible, place a shelf below the turkey to catch the fat and juices that will run off.

2 Check the temperature of the bird after two hours. Insert the temperature probe in the thickest part of the breast and into the lower part of the thigh. If the skin seems dry, add a dish of hot water on a tray below the turkey to increase the moisture levels within the smoker.

3 When the internal temperature of the turkey has reached 74°C (165°F), remove the bird from the smoker, wrap it in foil, and allow it to rest for an hour before carving.

Place the brined turkey in the hot smoker.

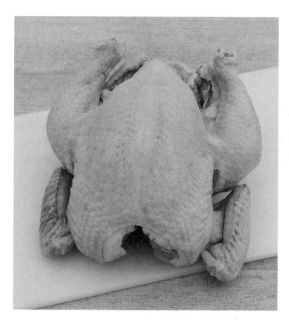

After brining, dry the turkey and leave it to rest.

A SWEET THOUGHT

To give your smoked turkey some extra sweetness, you can baste it in a mixture of 2 tablespoons of honey and 2 tablespoons of light soy sauce. Brush this mixture onto the skin after a few hours of smoking.

Smoking in Portions

To hot smoke turkey pieces, follow the steps for hot smoking chicken portions (page 188), but allow the meat to cook for a little longer in the smoker because of the larger size of the pieces. Hot-smoked turkey pieces can easily be kept in the freezer and used to make a flavourful casserole.

Turkey Pie with Vegetables

Hot smoked turkey is superb at Christmas served in traditional fashion with seasonal vegetables, stuffing, and cranberry sauce. And the leftovers are also delicious in your favourite chicken pie recipe. Serve with green beans or steamed broccoli.

HOT-SMOKED GOOSE

In many countries goose is the traditional centrepiece of the Christmas meal. And it is once again gaining popularity. Goose has a flavour similar to duck, and it also smokes beautifully.

In days gone by, goose was a popular bird for festive occasions, and would adorn many tables at Christmas time. A goose can be quite large, weighing in at around 4–7 kg (10–16 lb). Some domesticated breeds have been selectively bred to reach weights up to 10 kg (22 lb). Although large, geese can be smoked whole. Farmed geese are generally killed at around nine months and their flesh is likely to be tender. Wild geese are likely to be a little tougher and leaner than farmed birds. Goose is rarely sold in pieces but some specialist suppliers may allow you to purchase a crown (both breasts on the bone) or a couple of legs.

Full of Fat

Goose is a fatty bird and about 15 per cent of its fresh weight is made up of fat. Much of this is in a layer under the skin and drains out during cooking and can be saved. Goose fat is lower in saturates than pork fat and can be used as a healthier substitute in cooking and roasting. It is unmatched for roasting potatoes as it has a reasonably high smoke point of 190°C (375°F) and imparts a lovely flavour. During the hot-smoking process, some fat will be rendered from the bird, and you'll need to collect it. The presence of fat seeping through the meat during cooking preserves its moistness.

Smoking Times and Temperature

As when hot smoking all large birds, the watchwords are "low and slow". You'll need to keep a keen eye on temperature during smoking.

For a 7 kg (15½ lb) bird, the smoking time is about five or six hours depending on the temperature capabilities of your smoker. If you find it difficult to maintain a smoker temperature of 110°C (230°F), you'll need to extend the smoking time accordingly.

Whatever the temperature in the smoker happens to be, there will be a considerable lag in the temperature of the meat (internally). This is perfectly normal and will be the same for any meat cooked in an oven or smoker. This is why when food is cooked too quickly, the outside gets burned while the inside remains undercooked. In addition to the temperature lag, the energy in the smoker will be used to raise the temperature of the fat to render it down. I've sometimes cut away all the excess fat from around the neck and back end and also the whole skin section from the back. Most of the fat on a goose is inside the cavity or under the skin so it's easy to remove any excess. Remember to keep any fat you remove for roasting potatoes later.

The uniquely rich flavour of smoked goose needs no more complicated accompaniment than simply steamed or boiled potatoes.

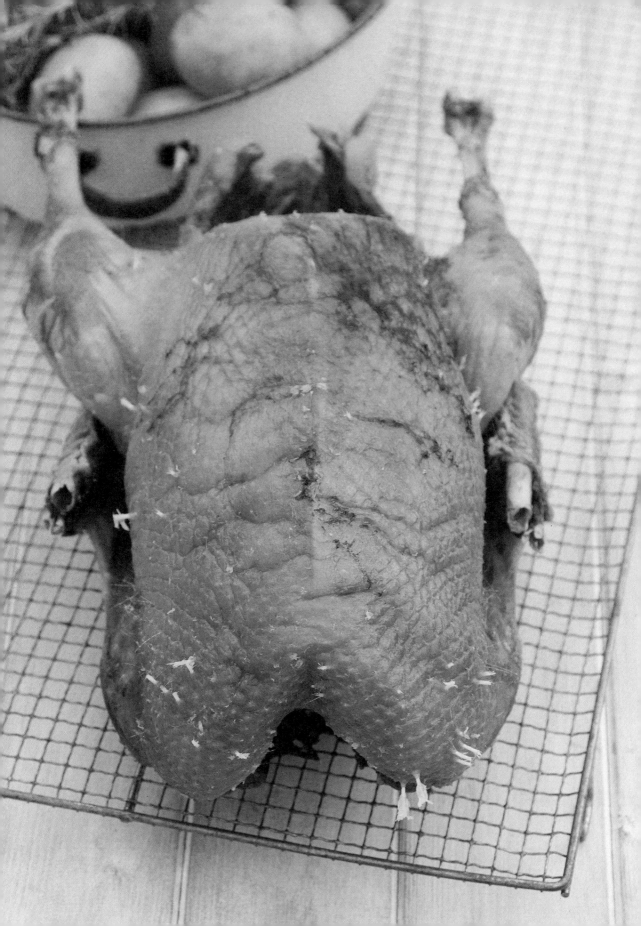

Pre-brining the Goose

1 In a nonreactive container large enough to hold the goose, mix up a 20 per cent SAL scale brine solution (see page 28). You can add sweeteners or some herbs and spices to the brine but make sure you dissolve all the salt first. Mix all the ingredients together and stir until all the salt has dissolved into the water. Chill the brine to 4°C (39°F).

2 Immerse the goose in the chilled brine so that the bird is completely submerged and check no air is trapped in the cavity. You may need to rest a plate or some other weight on top of the bird to ensure it remains submerged. It may be easier to immerse the bird breast-side down as this presents a flatter surface for a weight to rest upon.

3 Brine the goose in the refrigerator for 12 hours and then remove the bird from the brine. Drain the inside and pat the whole bird dry with kitchen paper. Allow the goose to rest at ambient temperature for an hour to allow it to warm through a little before it goes in the smoker.

Hot Smoking

1 Pre-heat the smoker to 110°C (230°F). Put the goose on a wire rack inside the smoker. Place a dish or bowl on a lower shelf under the goose to catch any rendered fat that will run off the bird during smoking.

2 Check the internal temperature of the goose after two hours by inserting a meat thermometer into the thickest part of the breast and into the bottom portion of the thigh. Check the condition of the skin and if it seems to be dry, add a dish of hot water on a tray below the goose to increase the moisture within the smoker.

3 When the goose has reached an internal temperature in excess of 74°C (165°F), remove it from the smoker, wrap it in foil, and allow to rest for an hour before serving.

TIP

The rendered goose fat from the smoker solidifies when cool. You can keep it in jars in the refrigerator for several months.

YOU WILL NEED
- **5 ½–7 kg (12–15 ½ lb) goose**
- **Salt**

Allow the brined goose to rest for an hour.

Place the goose in a pre-heated smoker.

Festive Smoked Goose

Hot-smoked goose is a real treat and one that you will remember for a long time. This rich and flavour-filled meat provides a real festive feast. Roasted apples make an interesting combination with goose. The acidity of the sharper-tasting varieties of apple works well with goose and cuts through the natural oils in goose meat.

METHOD

After the goose has been smoking for 1 hour, put a variety of vegetables in the oven to roast. Celery, carrots, parsnips, and fennel all work exquisitely with goose, as well as generous portions of potatoes. All these vegetables can be roasted in the fat that has been released from the goose. Richly coloured slow-braised red cabbage also goes very well with goose.

Be careful to select the tartest red apples and don't over roast the apples or they will disintegrate into apple sauce; roast apple quarters for about 20 minutes or whole apples for 35–40 minutes. Serve the smoked goose with the cooked apples, slices of orange, and cranberries or redcurrant jelly. You can also add a few spoons of redcurrant jelly to the gravy to add sweetness and acidity.

HOT-SMOKED DUCK BREAST

Exquisite when lightly smoked over fruit wood and sliced thinly, duck breasts are at their best when cooked to the point where they are still slightly pink in the middle. Succulent slices of smoked duck breast will transform a salad and can hold their own alongside the best charcuterie.

KEY STAGES

1 Preparation

2 Pre-brining

3 Pan frying

4 Smoking

The technique for smoking a whole duck is similar to that used for other poultry, but there are some wide variations in the seasonings you may wish to use. I recommend pre-brining to enhance the flavour and provide the opportunity to add some additional seasoning.

Smoke and Flavourings

While the smoky taste should be the main event, the presence of some background flavours will complement the duck and smoke combination. It's easy to add a variety of seasonings as part of a dry rub after brining. Duck works really well with exotic spices such as star anise, cloves, cinnamon, and ginger. But be sure not to apply these so heavily that they overpower the duck.

Controlling the Temperature

Duck breasts have quite a thick layer of fat under the skin, which can sometimes become a little dry. The skin can be hot smoked low-and-slow, which will help keep the fat moist and succulent, but the target temperature won't render the fat from under the skin. To reduce the fat, you can sear the skin in a hot frying pan for two minutes before hot smoking.

TIP

• Trim the duck and remove any silver skin on the meat side before brining.

• To add a little zing to your hot-smoked duck breasts, dust a teaspoon of Chinese five spice seasoning onto the flesh side of the duck breasts before brining. This will penetrate the meat, giving a hint of exotic spices to complement the smoke.

Preparing the Duck Breasts

1 Neaten the edges of the skin of the duck breasts. Remove any silver skin on the exposed meat side.

2 Make up about 1 litre (2 pints) of 80 per cent (SAL scale) brine solution in a nonreactive bowl (see page 28) and immerse the duck breasts in the brine for 20 minutes.

3 Remove the duck from the brine and rinse under cold running water. Pat dry with kitchen paper and place the duck breasts on a wire rack skin side up. Allow to dry in the refrigerator for about four hours.

Succulent sliced smoked duck breast, garnished with orange zest, is a mouth-watering addition to a charcuterie board.

Pan Frying

1 Heat a frying pan until it is very hot. Place the breasts skin side down in the pan for no longer than a minute. This will caramelize and crisp the skin, and render some of the fat. The added colour and complex flavours developed from the caramelized skin will work really well with the flavours produced by the smoke.

2 Remove the breasts from the pan and pat the skin with kitchen paper to remove some of the fat.

Smoking

1 The duck breasts are now ready to hot smoke. Remember that these breasts have only had the skin seared on one side and therefore require further heating to cook them through. Place the duck breasts on a wire rack ready to go into the smoker. Preheat the hot smoker to 110°C (230°F). I would use a fruit wood but if you prefer a darker colour for the finished product you can get excellent results with oak.

2 Hot smoke the duck breasts until the thickest part reaches over 74°C (165°F). Then remove the duck from the smoker and allow to cool on the wire rack. The cooling process firms up the meat so that it slices well. What's more, some of the harsher smoky notes dissipate during cooling.

Pan fry the duck breasts skin side down.

CRISPING THE SKIN AFTER SMOKING

You may prefer to crisp up the skin of the duck by pan frying after hot smoking. The disadvantage of this is that you risk overcooking the meat. If you choose to pan fry after smoking, it is best to allow the duck to cool completely before you put it in the hot pan.

Place the duck breasts on a rack in the smoker.

Hot-Smoked Duck and Noodle Salad

This is one of my favourite ways of serving hot-smoked duck breast. It brings together a delicious and simple medley of vegetables and flavourings. This dish makes a great starter and can be expanded into a more substantial dish by increasing the quantity of noodles used.

METHOD

The ingredients and quantities for this dish are very flexible and you can easily substitute seasonal alternatives to those suggested here. Simply fold thin slices of hot-smoked duck breast into a salad made with cooled cooked noodles, sliced peppers, mixed salad leaves, bean sprouts, finely chopped ginger and spring onions, and crushed walnuts. Dress with sesame oil and lemon juice.

HOT-SMOKED RABBIT

Rabbit is a healthy lean meat which takes the smoke really well and imparts a lovely flavour to stews and casseroles. Rabbit is an inexpensive alternative to chicken that is easy to prepare and hot smoke.

Rabbits have been hunted for centuries and wild populations exist in many countries around the world. Their meat is delicate and lean. Rabbits are abundant in the wild in many parts of the UK and are also farmed in some areas. They are usually easy to come by.

Smoking Considerations

Once butchered, rabbit is presented as a skinless carcass. This can present some challenges especially if you intend to cook it over an open fire or barbecue as there is a likelihood it will dry out without the natural protection of a layer of fat or skin. The same is also true when hot smoking as the process can take a relatively long time.

Maintaining Moisture

One very good way of protecting the rabbit while it is being smoked is to rub the surface of the carcass with oil or goose fat. This will act to retard the rate of moisture loss and will baste the rabbit at the same time as it cooks in the smoker. Adding a coating of oil will also help the smoke to adhere to the surface.

Adding Flavour

Using oil to help the smoking process and protect the rabbit is a real bonus. Another way in which oil or goose fat can complement the smoking process is as a means of applying extra flavourings to the rabbit. All you need to do is mix in a teaspoon of your chosen herb or spice mix (see Flavour Choices, left) into about four tablespoons of oil or goose fat. As the rabbit smokes in the hot environment of the smoker, the oil or fat will baste the meat and keep it moist.

FLAVOUR CHOICES

You can use a variety of store-cupboard staples to flavour hot-smoked rabbit. Just be sure that whatever flavours you use will work with that of the smoke. Most herbs are compatible but exercise caution when using aromatic spices as these don't always work well with smoke. A mixture of paprika and black pepper is one of my favourites, but with experience you can create your own flavour combinations.

The delicate flavour of hot-smoked rabbit works well with a simple pasta and salad accompaniment. A dab of chutney provides a piquant accent.

Pre-brining

1 In a nonreactive container, mix up a 20 per cent SAL scale brine solution (see page 28). You can add sweeteners or some herbs and spices into the brine but make sure you dissolve all the salt first. Mix all the ingredients together and stir. Chill the brine to 4°C (39°F) before immersing the rabbit.

2 Immerse the rabbit in the brine. Make sure it is completely submerged with no trapped air pockets. You may need to rest a plate or some other weight on top to ensure it stays submerged.

3 Brine the rabbit in the refrigerator for six hours and then remove it from the brine, drain, and pat the flesh dry with kitchen paper. If you want to cold smoke the rabbit, start the smoking at this stage (see Cold-Smoked Rabbit, below).

Smoking

1 Smear a little vegetable oil or goose fat over the carcass. Pre-heat the smoker to 85°C (185°F). Hang the rabbit from hooks in the smoker.

2 Check the rabbit after half an hour. If it is looking a little dry add a dish of hot water on a tray below to increase the moisture levels within the smoker.

3 When the rabbit has reached an internal temperature in excess of 74°C (165°F) remove it from the smoker, wrap it in foil, and allow it to rest for 20 minutes before serving.

Hang the rabbit in the smoker.

Place a dish of water in the smoker.

COLD-SMOKED RABBIT

If you would prefer to cold smoke your rabbit, after pre-brining simply place the rabbit in a cold smoker for 12 hours. The cold-smoked rabbit can then be cooked in the oven or used to make a tasty stew.

Smoked Rabbit Stew

Rabbit is a light meat with lots of flavour that, combined with vegetables, makes a fantastic stew. Rabbit should always be stewed on the bone to provide a really flavourful stock.

INGREDIENTS

- Whole hot-smoked rabbit (jointed)
- 4 large shallots (finely chopped)
- 2 medium carrots (finely chopped)
- 1 stick of celery (finely chopped)
- 10 pitted black olives
- 2 medium potatoes (sliced thinly)
- 10 cherry tomatoes
- 2 sprigs of rosemary
- 2 cloves of garlic (finely chopped)
- 1 tsp. cracked black pepper
- 3 tbsp. olive oil
- 2 tbsp. plain flour
- 250 ml (½ pint) white wine
- 250 ml (½ pint) water
- 1 chicken stock cube
- Salt and pepper to taste

Serves 4

METHOD

1 Coat the smoked rabbit joints in the flour mixed with salt and pepper. Brown in a deep pan with olive oil. Remove from the pan and set aside.

2 Fry the chopped shallots, garlic, celery, and carrots in the pan until soft. Stir in the wine and water, and add the chicken stock cube. Bring to the boil and add the potatoes and one of the sprigs of rosemary.

3 Add the rabbit, black olives, tomatoes, and remaining rosemary to the pan. Cover the pan and place in an oven preheated to 180°C (350°F) for 30 minutes. Remove the lid and continue to bake for 15 minutes until the tomotoes begin to brown. Serve with green beans.

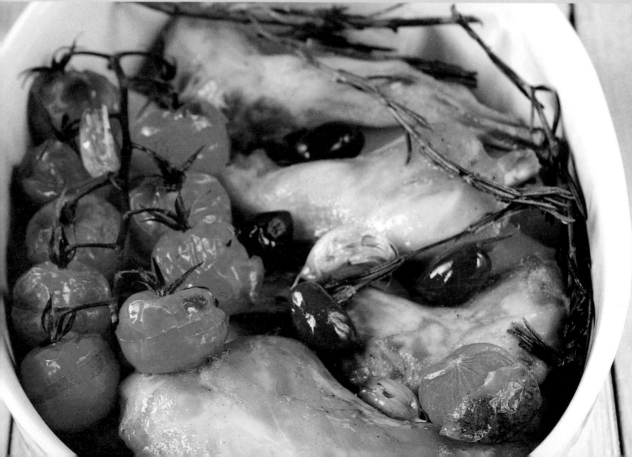

HOT-SMOKED VENISON

Venison – meat from deer – is rich in colour and very lean, having a low fat content. It beautifully complements the delicate smoky aroma produced by fruit woods, and once treated with smoke can be served in a variety of delicious ways.

KEY STAGES

1 Brining

2 Smoking

Searing the outside of the venison before smoking preserves the attractive dark colour of the meat.

There are many breeds of deer and the term venison is applied to the meat from all of these. Venison from farmed deer is often sold ready butchered and skinned from specialist suppliers. It is very low in fat and cholesterol compared with other red meats.

Smoking Considerations

Low in fat, venison has little natural protection from drying when hot smoked. It therefore needs to be smoked using a variety of techniques to keep it moist. Pre-brining is essential and moisture can also be preserved by raising the humidity in the smoker. This can be done quite simply by placing a pan of warm water in the smoker (usually at a lower level than the food being smoked).

Brine Strength

Pre-brining venison is a straightforward way of ensuring that moisture is retained when the meat is smoked. This can be done using a weak brine solution of around 40 per cent (SAL scale). See the brine tables on page 28 to calculate the amount of salt for a given quantity of water for making brine. Brining in a weak solution can be an advantage if you want to add herbs or sweeteners to the brine; the meat can spend longer in a weak solution to take on the flavours without becoming too salty. The meat needs to be prepared for brining so it can benefit from immersion in the brine. Deer are active animals and, while there is little fat to trim from the meat, there is quite a lot of connective tissue and silverskin on the meat surface, which can stop the brine from penetrating the flesh. All this needs to be removed to leave a dark, lean piece of muscle.

Adding Colour

The hot-smoking process can leave venison looking a little pale. This is because as the meat cooks through in the gentle heat, it doesn't undergo the caramelization process that occurs when the meat is fried. One way to get over this is to flash fry the venison in a lightly oiled, searingly hot frying pan for 30 seconds on each side after brining and before hot smoking. For larger cuts, you will need to use a barbecue to sear the meat (see page 210). After frying and hot smoking, the meat has an appetizing, deep colour and a satisfying, complex flavour. Lightly coating the surface of the meat with oil is a great way to encourage the smoke to stick to the meat to achieve maximum flavour.

Smoking Time

If you are smoking a large piece of venison, say 3–6 kg (7–13 lb), you should set the temperature of the smoker to 110–120°C (225–250°F). This temperature is sufficient to penetrate and cook the meat over time. If the temperature in the smoker is much lower, there is a chance your venison won't reach the necessary internal temperature. If you're hot smoking a smaller piece of venison, you can use a lower temperature, about 90–95°C (195–203°F).

ALTERNATIVE FLAVOURS

The basic brine for curing venison in is just water and salt, but you can add flavours and sweeteners to the brine to provide an extra dimension. But make sure that any flavours you choose don't overpower the flavour and aroma of the smoke. The following quantities are for 1 litre (2 pints) of brine. If you need more brine to cover your meat, just increase the quantities of the salt and water and other liquid ingredients. Herbs and spices can be increased a little, but there is no need to increase these in proportion to the brine.

SWEET JUNIPER AND HERB
10 juniper berries (crushed)
1 tsp. dried thyme
3 tbsp. sugar

TRADITIONAL HERB AND GARLIC
1 tsp. dried thyme
1 tsp. dried sage
1 tsp. dried rosemary
2 cloves of garlic (crushed)
2 tbsp. honey

SWEET CHILLI AND TERIYAKI
1 tsp. chilli flakes
2 tbsp. paprika
4 tbsp. teriyaki sauce
2 tbsp. honey

Pre-Brining

1 Prepare the meat by removing all the sinew and silverskin from the surface of the meat. Mix the brine solution in a nonreactive container that is large enough to hold the meat immersed in brine. Make up a suffcent quantity of 40 per cent brine (SAL scale) (see page 28). Chill the brine to 4°C (40°F). At this point you can add herbs, spices, and sweeteners as suggested on page 209.

2 Immerse the meat in the brine making sure it is completely covered and leave it to stand for up to 6 hours for a whole hind leg or 2 hours for a piece 50 mm (2 in) in thickness. After the allotted time, remove the venison from the brine and pat it dry with kitchen paper. There is no need to rinse the meat.

Searing and Smoking

1 Lightly rub the meat with vegetable oil and fry the venison in a pre-heated pan for 30 seconds on each side. If you are working with a really large piece of venison you can sear the meat on a barbecue.

2 Pre-heat the smoker to 90–95°C (195–203°F) for a small piece of venison or, for a whole hind leg, 110–120°C (225–250°F). Choose apple wood for a sweet finish to the meat or, if you prefer a stronger flavour, you can use oak or whisky oak, which adds a special kick to the finished meat.

3 Smoke the venison until the internal temperature (measured with a meat thermometer) exceeds 74°C (165°F). If you are working with a particularly large piece of venison it may be necessary to increase the temperature of the smoker to achieve the internal temperature of the meat; 150°C (300°F) will get the job done, but take care to prevent the venison from drying out. Remove the venison from the smoker and allow it to rest for an hour.

Remove all visible fat and sinew from the venison.

Fry the venison in a hot pan for a short time.

Place the oiled venison in a hot smoker.

Hot-Smoked Venison Salad with Pomegranate Dressing

The wild, earthy flavour and smoky notes of this meat work exceptionally well with a fresh salad dressed with an unusual fruity vinaigrette. The salad can be made with your choice of seasonal salad leaves and herbs, and is easy to assemble.

INGREDIENTS

- 450 g (1 lb) hot-smoked venison (cooled)
- Seasonal salad leaves and fresh herbs
- 8 radishes
- 1 lemon (sliced)

FOR THE DRESSING:

- 2 tbsp. pomegranate vinegar
- 1 tsp. wholegrain mustard
- 1 tsp. clear honey
- 1 tbsp. light soy sauce
- ½ clove of garlic (crushed)
- Pinch of salt

Serves 4

METHOD

1 To make the dressing, grind the garlic and salt to a fine paste using a pestle and mortar. Add the vinegar and stir until the salt is completely dissolved. Mix in the soy sauce, honey, and wholegrain mustard. Add a dash of water to loosen the dressing.

2 Slice the smoked venison thinly. This is easiest to do when the venison is cool. Divide the salad leaves and herbs into four bowls. Arrange the venison slices on top and add the radishes and slices of lemon as a garnish. Serve the dressing on the side.

Resources

GLOSSARY

Aitch bone The bone that forms part of the pig's hip, which contains the socket for the femur.

Anaerobic bacteria Bacteria that have the ability to thrive in low oxygen conditions.

Ascorbic acid A chemical, otherwise known as vitamin C, that is sometimes used alongside other curing salts, especially in bacon cures. It acts to inhibit the formation of nitrosamines.

Baby back ribs The portion of ribs cut from the upper part of the pig's ribs near the loin.

Baume scale Also termed degrees Baume (B°), this scale measures the percentage of salt by weight and reads from 0 B° for fresh water up to 26.4 B° for a completely saturated brine.

Blood line The medial vein in the gut cavity of a fish next to the spine. It is usually identified by its dark colour.

Boston Butt The upper part of the shoulder of a pig. This cut can include the collar and the shoulder blade.

Botulism A serious condition caused by a toxin produced by the bacterium *Clostridium botulinum.*

Brine A solution of salt in water used for curing meat or fish (see Brining). Sweeteners, vinegars, spices, and herbs, can be added.

Brining The process of immersing meat or fish in brine to add flavour and/or preserve the food.

Brining pump A syringe-like device used for injecting brine into meat (see Injection brining).

Brisket A cut of beef taken from the lower chest or breast of the cow.

Butcher's knot A constricting slip knot used for securing rolls of meat or boned cuts of meat.

Butcher's netting An elasticated mesh stocking that is used to hold meat in shape while roasting or drying. Butcher's netting is food grade and heat resistant. It can sometimes be used as an alternative to butcher's string.

Butcher's string A strong, food-grade rayon twine. Used for tying cuts of meat for roasting, brining, or drying.

Case hardening A term used in relation to air drying meat, when the outer part of the meat has dried too rapidly and formed a dry layer on the outer part of the meat thereby inhibiting further drying.

Casing The outer skin of a sausage or salami. Casings can be made from animal intestines or can be made from collagen or other synthetic materials.

Charcuterie The term used to describe the practice of preparing, curing, and preserving meats, and also the products made using these techniques.

Clostridium botulinum A bacterium that produces a toxin that is dangerous to humans. It is naturally found in the environment and is present in soil. See also Botulism.

Cold smoking The process of using smoke to preserve and flavour food at temperatures below 30°C (86°F).

Combustion A chemical reaction in which fuel reacts rapidly with oxygen to produce heat.

Conditioning room A room that is used to air dry and condition meat or fish, incorporating mechanisms to regulate temperature and humidity.

Curing A preservation process in which dry salt or salt solution (see Brine) is applied to meat or fish.

Damper A device that is used to adjust the airflow through a smoker and can be found on either the smoker itself or the fire box (if a remote smoke source is being used). Its main purpose is to allow slowing of the combustion process to assist in the production of smoke. Where the damper is not adjustable, it is referred to as a passive damper.

Dehydrator A machine that combines gentle heat and air movements to dry food on racks. Usually powered electrically, it can incorporate a timer and other controls.

Desiccation The process of drying or removing water from a substance.

Dredging A method of applying dry salt to meat when curing. The meat is simply covered in salt. Sometimes referred to as the salt box method.

Dry-aging bag A plastic bag made from a breathable plastic that allows moisture to pass through it. These bags can be used for drying or aging meats in the refrigerator without the need for expensive conditioning rooms.

Dry salting The process of applying dry salt to a piece of meat or fish to cure it.

Drying To reduce the moisture content in a given foodstuff. This reduction in water content can be achieved in the open air or by the use of heat and fans or a combination of both. See also Desiccation.

Escherichia coli A species of bacteria that normally live in the intestines of humans and animals. Most varieties are harmless or cause relatively brief diarrhoea, but some more virulent strains can result in more serious sickness.

Equalization brining A brining technique in which the brine strength is calculated in such a way as to prevent over brining.

Fat cap The layer of subcutaneous fat that is found on some cuts of meat, escpecially around the back, loin, and leg of a pig.

Fermented sausage A sausage that has been treated with live bacterial culture to promote fermentation to add flavour. These sausages require careful preparation, monitoring, and drying conditions to achieve good results.

Foil packet A means of producing smoke on a barbecue in which wood chips are wrapped in foil.

Ham Salt-cured pork meat. The term ham is also used for other meats that have been cured in a similar way, for example, duck ham.

Hot smoking The process of using smoke to flavour food while applying heat to cook the food at the same time.

Immersion brining A technique for curing food that involves covering the food completely in a brine solution, usually using a deep container or bucket.

Injection brining A method of hastening the curing process. The brine is injected into the meat using a brining pump.

Kosher salt A type of salt used in curing and brining characterized by its angular sharp grains that help the cure to penetrate the meat.

Listeria monocytogenes A species of bacteria that can cause serious health problems in humans.

Loin The muscle group that runs either side of the spine any four-legged animal.

Meat thermometer A temperature probe for checking the internal temperature of meat or fish during cooking. Usually oven proof.

Nitrates Chemicals (usually potassium nitrate) used in very small quantities in the production of cured meats. Their presence helps prevent spoilage and also maintains the red colour in muscle tissue.

Nitrites Chemicals (usually sodium nitrite) used in very small quantities in the production of cured meats. Sodium nitrite is effective against *Clostridium botulinum* bacteria, which release the toxin that causes botulism.

Nitrosamines A group of compounds formed in cured meats when nitrites are converted to nitric oxide, nitrosonium, and water. The nitrosonium reacts with constituents of the meat proteins to form nitrosamines. These compounds have the potential to cause cancer when consumed in large quantities. This potential is reduced by the addition of ascorbic acid (see above) to the curing mix.

Off-set smoking A hot-smoking technique in which the food is placed so that it does not receive direct heat from the heat source (usually charcoal) and therefore cooks more gently than would otherwise be the case.

Ox runner A large natural casing taken from the cow's large intestine, sometimes referred to as ox bung. It is used for making large dry-cured sausages and other cured meats.

PDV salt Pure dried vacuum salt, a refined and dried salt that may contain an anticaking agent to maintain its free flowing characteristics.

Pellicle A thin, sticky film that forms on the surface of cured meat or fish, which helps the smoke stick to the surface.

Prague Powder A proprietary blend of salts used for the preservation of meat. There are two types: Prague Powder #1 and Prague Powder #2.

Pre-brining The process of immersing meat or fish into a brine solution as a first step in a curing process. (See also Brining.)

Pyrolysis The decomposition of a fuel by the application of heat. Usually associated with indirect heating and doesn't rely the presence of oxygen.

Relative humidity (RH) The ratio of the amount of water vapour in the air at a specific temperature to the maximum amount that the air could hold at that temperature. RH is expressed as a percentage.

Render To remove fat from meat by the application of heat either through roasting, hot smoking, or frying in a pan or skillet.

SAL A measure used to express the amount of salt in a brine solution in a scale from 0 to 100.

Salami A term for an Italian cured and fermented spiced sausage using various meats but usually pork. See also Fermented sausage.

Salometer A device for measuring the salt content of a brine solution.

Salt See Sodium chloride.

Saltpetre The common name for potassium nitrate, a chemical used used as a long-term preservative. See Nitrates.

Saturated A term used to describe a brine solution that has the maximum amount of salt dissolved into the water. A saturated brine solution cannot dissolve any more salt and any added salt will remain in crystal form.

Sausage stuffer A mechanical device for stuffing sausages. These can be attached to food mixers or hand-operated meat grinders. Dedicated sausage stuffers usually comprise a cylinder and piston with a mechanical crank handle to push the meat through a tube into the casing.

Searing The term given to frying meat in a very hot frying pan to brown the meat or to render fat.

Smoke The product of combustion or pyrolysis. It contains many chemical compounds that provide flavour and aroma and some of which assist in the preservation of food.

Smoke pipe A pipe used to transmit smoke from the source of the smoke to the smoking cabinet.

Smoke spreader A device that usually comprises a flat barrier with holes or slots in its surface. A smoke spreader is usually installed low down in the smoking compartment to encourage the smoke to spread out across the whole area of the smoker.

Smoking The process of applying smoke to food to add flavour and/or preserve it.

Smouldering A combustion process that produces no flames, consumes fuel slowly, and releases low levels of heat.

Sodium chloride The chemical name for common salt (chemical formula NaCl). The application of salt is a key part of the food preservation processes described in this book.

Spare ribs The lower ribs of the pig cut from the where they meet at the sternum.

Target temperature A method of hot smoking meat or fish in which the smoker heat is set to a high temperature and the food is smoked until it reaches a specified internal temperature rather than leaving it in the smoker for a specific length of time.

Trotter The foot of a pig.

Vacuum packing A method of storing food that extends its keeping qualities by means of a machine that removes the air from within a specially designed food-safe plastic bag. This prevents oxidation of the food, which can then be stored in a refrigerator or freezer.

Water pan A pan of water placed in a hot smoker to maintain humidity during a long hot smoking process. The water in the pan prevents the food from overdrying and helps to stabilize the heat levels in the smoker.

Wood chips Wood pieces or particles larger than 3 mm (1/8 in) in diameter.

Wood dust Wood particles smaller than 3 mm (1/8 in) in diameter and often much smaller.

SUPPLIERS

The following listing includes major suppliers of equipment, materials, and accessories related to the techniques described in this book.

It is not exhaustive and, with a little research, you may find an excellent supplier for your needs locally.

SMOKERS AND BARBECUE GRILLS

Arden Smokers' Supplies
www.foodsmoker.co.uk
01364 644965

Bradley Smokers
www.bradleysmoker.co.uk
01803 712712

Cookequip Ltd
www.cookequip.co.uk
01932 841171

For Food Smokers
www.forfoodsmokers.co.uk
01483 550694

Hot Smoked
www.hotsmoked.co.uk
01398 351604

Mac's BBQ
www.macsbbq.com
01208 75385

Napoleon Grills
www.napoleongrills.co.uk
01676 522788

Planet Barbeque
www.planetbarbeque.co.uk
01271 378887

Weber BBQ
www.weberbbq.co.uk
01756 692611

CURING SALTS AND INGREDIENTS

Alderson Ingredients
www.aldersoningredients.co.uk
01908 951419

Scobie & Junor Ltd
www.scobiesdirect.com
0800 783 7331

Smokedust
www.smokedust.co.uk
01908 661848

Weschenfelder
www.weschenfelder.co.uk
01642 241 395

SausageMaking.org
www.sausagemaking.org
0845 643 6915

Sausage Kings
www.sausage-kings.co.uk
Tel: 01530 272396

KITCHEN EQUIPMENT AND ACCESSORIES

Cream Supplies
www.creamsupplies.co.uk
0845 226 3024

Joynsons
www.joynsons.com
01482 320622

Nisbets
www.nisbets.co.uk
0845 140 5555

Parkers Food Machinery Plus
www.pfmplus.co.uk
0844 980 2438

SALT SEASONINGS AND SPICES

A W Smiths
www.awsmith.co.uk
0121 486 4500

British Salt Limited
www.british-salt.co.uk
01606 839250

Peacock Salt
www.peacocksalt.com
01292 292000

FOOD DEHYDRATORS

UK Juicers
www.ukjuicers.com
01904 757070

KNIVES

Cutting Edge Knives
www.cuttingedgeknives.co.uk
01484 817423

Kin Knives
www.kinknives.com
01394 461075

Soho Knives
www.sohoknives.com
01372 220926

BOOKS AND PUBLICATIONS

Local Food Heroes
www.localfoodheroes.co.uk

The British Barbeque Society
www.bbbqs.com

Food Standards Agency
www.food.gov.uk
020 7210 4850

INDEX

Figures in *italic* type refer to photographs.

Classic salami page 116

ACKNOWLEDGEMENTS

Quantum Publishing would like to thank the following for supplying images for inclusion in this book:

30: oliveromg/Shutterstock.com; 33: Steve Brown Photography/Getty Images; 41: Jamie Rogers/Shutterstock.com; 44: funkyfrogstock/Shutterstock.com; 55: Katerina Belaya/Shutterstock.com; 61: istetiana/Shutterstock.com; 72: BrunoRosa/Shutterstock.com; 102: B. and E. Dudzinscy/Shutterstock.com; 103: AleksandarMilutinovic/Shutterstock.com; 104: margouillat photo/Shutterstock.com; 105: Kondor83/Shutterstock.com; 109: A_Lein/Shutterstock.com; 123: Wiktory/Shutterstock.com; 125: Martin Turzak/Shutterstock.com; 128: Olga Nayashkova/Shutterstock.com; 132: Winfried Heinze/Getty Images; 157: Evgeny Litvinov/Shutterstock.com; 160: margouillat photo/Shutterstock.com; 162: Howard Shooter/Getty Images; 171: Huw Jones/Getty Images; 175: Anna Hoychuk/Shutterstock.com; 179: Diana Miller/Getty Images; 183: Sam Stowell/Getty Images; 199: Shebeko/Shutterstock.com; 203: Simone Voigt/Shutterstock.com; 207: Lucky_elephant/Shutterstock.com; 211: Contrail/Shutterstock.com; 195 (top): Elena Shashkina/Shutterstock.com; 195 (below): DimaP/Shutterstock.com

All other images are the copyright of Quantum Publishing. Thanks to Turan for the illustrations on pages 68, 135, 140, 141, 142, 143, 147, 151 and the photograph on page 99. All other photography by Simon Pask.

While every effort has been made to credit contributors, Quantum Publishing would like to apologise should there have been any omissions or errors and would be pleased to make the appropriate correction to future editions of the book.

Thanks to the US Consultant for his careful work on the book: Matthew McClune, Ogeechee Meat Market, Savannah, GA. OgeecheeMeatMarket.com

Author's acknowledgements

Researching and writing this book has been a real journey, giving me and my family the opportunity to try out some truly delicious food, rediscover some of my favourite charcuterie, and write down my recipes for others to discover and enjoy for themselves. Writing this book has been made so much easier having the forensically methodical eye of my editor Cathy Meeus by my side who has made my words come to life on the page. Alongside us both there have been the team at Quantum Publishing with support and encouragement from Kerry Enzor, Sorrel Wood, and Sam Kennedy, who have worked so hard to bring this book the print. The imagery for this book has been expertly styled and shot by Simon Pask, who not only takes a great picture but has the patience of a saint to work through nine days of photo shoot with a novice writer. Thanks Simon.

Writing this book was an entirely new experience for me, and my family have supported me throughout. I have a passion for food and to have the opportunity to commit this passion to paper was a real honour. I would like to thank my wonderful wife Alison for all her support, encouragement, love, and patience throughout the writing of this book and for her unending patience in knowing that even with our wedding to plan I was given the space and time to sit and write to a deadline.

I would also like to thank my suppliers who have been there for me when I needed meat, fish, and poultry out of season. Special thanks to Woburn Country foods for supplying the bulk of the meats featured in this book. James at Pastures farm in Yardley Hastings for supplying me with game birds out of season. Mark Fairweather and Diego Antela, two very dedicated, competent fishmongers who know their trade and have gone out of their way to help me get the right fish when I needed them. William Yates from billyfranks.co.uk for supplying me with one of the best beef jerky recipes I've tasted. It's in the book and I encourage you to try it (Sweet and Sour Jerky, page 90). And finally I have to acknowledge my parents Ann and Seref Turan, who are no longer with us, for igniting my passion for food that endures to this day. Thank you.